R. TOMPSETT
FARM COTTAGE
STONEGATE
WADHURST
TN5 7EN
TELE: 01580 200428

R. TOMPSETT
FARM COTTAGE
STONEGATE
WADHURST
TN5 7EN
TELE: 01580 200428

WORKING WITH NATURE

Memoirs of a wildlife manager

Frontispiece:
Eskdalemuir, with H.R.H. Prince Charles and Captain Farquharson of Invercauld.

WORKING WITH NATURE

Memoirs of a wildlife manager

RONNIE ROSE M.B.E.

Foreword by Duff Hart-Davis

DAVID A H GRAYLING
2004

WORKING WITH NATURE
Memoirs of a wildlife manager

ISBN – 0 906839 04 1

Published by David A H Grayling
Shap, Penrith, Westmorland, England. CA10 3NG.

Printed in Great Britain by Antony Rowe Limited, Chippenham, Wiltshire.

FOREWORD

FORESTER and naturalist extraordinary, Ronnie Rose has unique knowledge of the Scottish Uplands. Having devoted his career to the grand hill country north of the border, and to the welfare of its wildlife, he knows the ways of every creature, from the smallest insect to the mighty golden eagle. Red deer and roe, red grouse, black grouse and capercaillie, salmon and trout, raptors and their prey – all have flourished under his care.

His lasting memorial will be the great forest which he created at Eskdalemuir, in Dumfries-shire, during the 1970s. Until then, it had been widely assumed that conifer plantations were inimical to birds and animals; but by his imaginative planting, and by incorporating deciduous trees and open spaces into his designs, Ronnie confounded the pessimists. He showed that well-planned and managed commercial woodland can support a huge variety of wildlife.

In this book – part autobiography, part practical instruction, part call for realistic wildlife policies – he tells absorbing stories of how he helped nature re-build broken food-chains and nurse threatened species back to health. Readers will be entranced, for instance, by his description of how he persuaded a colony of short-eared owls to shift its ground and deal with a plague of voles.

Always a man of strong opinions, he has often disconcerted critics by the vigour with which he puts forward his beliefs. Yet no one can doubt his sincerity: he has been closely involved with the land all his life, and his book is a powerful demand for commonsense in the management of the country that he loves.

Duff Hart-Davis 2004

ACKNOWLEDGEMENTS

MY special thanks to those who have provided me with photographs, paintings and drawings. This is a vital part of the book, as nature is a kaleidoscope of shapes and colours that can be frozen in time by brush, pen or camera. I have always illustrated my talks with slides, and owe a great dept of gratitude to all who have given these to me over the years. I have used some of these in this book; they were kindly donated by Ken McArthur, Emilio Dicerbo, Kenny Wright, Mike Budden, Bobbie Smith, Duncan Green (Tweed Foundation) and finally in remembrance of three good friends – Tom Griffen, Gareth Lewis (Buccleugh Estates) and Lea MacNally. Colin Beck Mackay took the photograph of me on the back of the jacket.

Most of the photographs were taken by the "Master" – Ken Taylor A.R.P.S. – and myself. He taught me how to use a camera, so I hope I have done him justice. Ken's wife Joan also deserves my gratitude for her skill and endless patience whilst locating our "subjects" hidden in the forest.

That fine artist Elizabeth Halstead specially painted for me the stag on the hill which adorns the dust jacket. I am most grateful to her for this, and her permission to use it. The painting of the red deer in the book is also hers. The line drawings were created by my daughter Yvonne.

My very sincere thanks to my family and friends with whom I share my vocational love for nature, as they form the heart of the book. It is only by sharing our experiences that we can develop that inner knowledge and respect for the flora and fauna which are essential to conservation. I feel blessed indeed to have shared with them so many priceless moments along the way. I look back with a mixture of gladness and sadness – glad to have met them and sad that so many have passed away to another place. When I return to those special places in the hills, they often return, prompted by a sight or sound, only to vanish on the wind, lost in the solitude of my surroundings.

Most of this book was scribbled on numerous writing pads as I sat on a hillside surrounded by nature. I am not a writer but I was determined to put my feelings on paper my way. My two daughters, Carolyn and Yvonne and son-in-law Jon transferred my notes to the word processor. Of course we soon found that it was too long and too outspoken, and my friends will know why. I was assured that this rough diamond could be polished without losing its value. So my special thanks go to my family and friends, Duff Hart-Davis, Michael Wigan, David Beevers, and David Grayling for providing the French polish, whilst ensuring that my passion for nature remained intact.

TO FLORENCE.

For her faith, wise counsel and support, but most of all
for sharing our love with my passion for nature.

x

CONTENTS

INTRODUCTION

FOR over 200 years the Rose family have been employed by kings, queens, dukes, barons and numerous estate owners to manage wildlife. The first record appears in an ancient book on deer forests and refers to Aeneas Rose, who was employed by the Duke of Atholl at the end of the 18th century. As well as acting as a deer stalker, he was the Duke's Pipe Major for his private army, the Atholl Highlanders. They played and danced for many notable people, including Napoleon and Queen Victoria, and this led to her employing my grandfather when she purchased Balmoral Estate in 1848.

As I travel up the A9 from Perth to Inverness, I often ponder on days long past as I look at the wonderful landscapes that have been created by forestry and wildlife management working together for the past two centuries and more, to fashion the magnificent countryside that so many of us in the family have laboured in and fought for.

I look at Blair Castle, which sits at the heart of it all, and try to imagine the thoughts of my predecessors. I am certain they never imagined as they walked through the Pass of Killiecrankie that, two generations later, in 1960, I would be instructing a course in wildlife management on the very same land, and that I would return there as a guest of HRH the Prince of Wales when he opened the Loch Tummel Wildlife Centre.

As my son and grandsons are now on the same career path, I wonder what they will find at Blair Atholl or Balmoral in the year 2060.

HISTORY 1870–1939

Chapter 1

HABITATS AND HERITAGE

THE first forests to cover our countryside evolved over thousands of years, fashioned by soil, seed, wind and weather. During this time the wildlife developed within new habitats, each animal or bird using various food-chains to form a natural balance of interdependent coexistence, which was beneficial to the survival of them all. The forests which spread over our uplands were a mixture of trees and shrubs of different hues and textures: deciduous and conifer creating light and darkness, food and shelter, and providing sustainable continuity.

It was only by a gradual process that man established domination over nature. This predatory animal – for that is what man often is – did not create devastation until much later. It would seem that the worst damage to most of our uplands has taken place only during the last 400 years, in the name of progress and improvement.

While man was spending much of his time and effort killing other men, his impact on the environment around him was not particularly detrimental – apart from the fact that he cut trees for building ships. Domestic clan warfare and conflicts abroad, for whatever reason, were actually beneficial to nature, because the countryside was left in peace. When man was slaughtering man, the population was being culled annually. Cholera, smallpox, famine and a host of other evils were all beneficial, contributory factors in population control.

Because travel was so difficult, the majority of people spent their lives within a small area, forming close relationships with each other and with the wildlife of the surrounding district. Their well-being depended on the soil, weather and seasonal changes, just like that of the birds and animals that lived around them. This interdependence created an understanding and respect for the land that is often missing from our modern society, with its over-indulgent material demands threatening environmental sustainability.

It is impossible to put a precise date on any one moment when humans changed the overall structure of the forest to such an extent that the natural balance could no longer maintain itself. Perhaps we could say that the first man to secure a sharp flint to a piece of wood and chop down a tree was the earliest vandal. At any rate, we know that somebody did this, and that, as a result, there are no natural areas of habitat left in our countryside. Man has moulded the landscape, and the environment that has evolved as a result requires on-going, active management by him.

The destruction has been slow but relentless, with each generation demanding more from the land. Just as the ebb and flow of the sea on the shore changes our coastline, so the passage of time and the demands of man progressed from south to north, from Lowlands to Highlands, with each new phase of rapacious behaviour destroying the natural forms of the land and gradually creating the patchwork of habitats that we have today.

The first major changes were influenced by weather. As the climate cooled and average temperature dropped, the predominance of broad-leaved, deciduous trees changed to a mixture of conifer and deciduous, with upland areas developing a particular preference for pine. Soil type, elevation and exposure are the three major influences governing the successful establishment and long-term survival of any woodland. As hill-farming expanded, the tree-cover diminished and the ground was exposed to the elements, so that at times of flood the rich soils on the hillsides were flushed into the valley bottoms or out to the sea. Consequently, many of the areas that were initially able to support the original forests are now impoverished. We still have the same type of climate, which is something those well-meaning but misled individuals who would like to see the Uplands from Land's End to John O'Groats covered in oak trees would do well to remember – unless of course they merely want a vast area of bonsai plants. They certainly will not produce natural woodland or a valuable habitat for wildlife.

We have a very mixed climate, wet, dry, hot and cold by turns, which is ideal for creating new conifer forests, but these must be designed and managed for the good of all those truly concerned with the countryside, and of those who live and earn their living there. The ideal forest is a mixture of young and old deciduous and conifer species, with grassland and heather all playing a part in the design.

Historical records chart the destruction of our natural woodlands and the reshaping of our countryside. Caledonian forests of Scots pine, ash, alder, birch and juniper were cut for domestic fuel and boat-building. Clearings in the forest were occupied by farmers with goats, cattle and horses, thus ensuring that the trees could not regenerate. Cultivation and burning were all part of the 'improvements' imposed upon the land. Gradually the forests were pushed back to the more remote parts of our country, mainly in the north. Alas, they were not safe even there, as the demand for iron smelting, salt production, wool and mutton eventually hastened the destruction of the remaining shrubs and natural woodlands.

The 1745 rebellion signalled the end of a way of life in the Scottish Uplands, where the local people were part of a clan, and each clan worked as an extended family, with their main wealth measured in numbers of black cattle. At the end of each summer thousands of beasts were taken off the hills and driven to the markets of Perth, Crieff and Stirling where they were sold to dealers from the south. Then Bonnie Prince Charlie – this young European with a royal pedigree – landed on the Hebrides with seven friends and set church against church, Scot against Scot. In the 250 years since then, nothing has changed, and the same kind of thing is happening all over the world today. It does not really matter whether you die on the receiving end of a claymore, a bayonet or an Exocet missile; the result is final. Unfortunately, man now has not only the means to kill his fellow man, but also the ability to destroy the world.

The persecution and plundering which took place after the battle of Culloden in 1746 destroyed the old Highland way of life, and by 1775 many of the hill people had decided it was time to leave. Unfortunately, the first migrants were some of the more able and better-educated members of the community. They had been mainly responsible for the daily management of affairs and were known as tax-men, since they were responsible for the local letting of the land. Lettings could be paid for by cash, animals or labour, so the managers were in positions of influence, and were able to pay passage on ships to North America or Canada, where they used their experience to establish well-run communities which are still there today. Unfortunately for Scotland, they were our first brain-drain, and the process is still continuing.

Black-faced sheep could flourish on the Uplands in spite of the harsh conditions, and there was a big demand for wool and mutton, so the rents charged to the small hill farmer or crofter were raised beyond his ability to pay. Huge areas were then cleared of humans. For the next 100 years the hills were white with sheep, and any remaining woodland was put to the torch. The only areas spared this rape were developed for sport. John Prebble's well-known book on the Highland clearances provides a vivid and interesting account of this period of Scottish history, which had a devastating effect on Upland habitats.

The first roads had been built by General Wade early in the eighteenth century, to help the English army of occupation get about the Highlands to supply food and equipment to its various garrisons. These highways were of little help to individual estates, most of which lay off the beaten track. The first substantial improvements came as a result of the genius of a man called Thomas Telford, born in the Uplands of south Scotland. With a labour force of men starving and destitute as a result of the Irish potato famine of 1846, he built roads and bridges all over the remoter parts of the countryside, providing the vital links that enabled estate owners to develop their own transport system of coaches to the remote glens.

Two main habitats were being created at this time, in order to produce the food-chains and environmental requirements of the principal sporting quarries, namely red grouse and red deer. The red grouse required heather of different ages, some short, some longer, and this was achieved by burning the moors in small patches. Regenerating native Scots pine was cut, grazed or burned, and all species of birds of prey, regardless of their diet, were shot on sight, trapped or poisoned. The red deer habitat was usually in the more mountainous regions, with a mixture of long heather and rough upland grasses. The more fertile valleys were cultivated to provide winter food for the deer, and native trees were planted to give them shelter and sanctuary.

The cost of labour was then so low that large numbers of staff could be employed to ensure that these habitats expanded, and access roads and hill paths were maintained to a high standard so that the best management practices could be carried out. By the second half of the 19th century, management for shooting had developed into a fine art. A variety of sports were practised on each Highland estate, according to the limitations of size, soil type, climate, and altitude. The smaller properties often specialised in roe deer and pheasants, but larger estates were in the more fortunate position of being able to offer red deer, grouse, black grouse, partridge, snipe and duck, providing a paradise for sportsmen. As each species of animal and bird needed a different habitat, large parts of the most beautiful landscapes which are now major tourist attractions were created at this time.

The disadvantage of red deer stalking was that the sportsman had to be fit enough to walk up to fifteen a miles a day. The number of sportsmen that any estate could take depended on its size, with one rifle a day on each beat. The price of shooting smaller game came within the reach of more and more people, but stalking remained more specialised and mostly for the richer person, or the fortunate friends of those who owned deer forests. This is no longer the case, because stalking can now be obtained for a small fraction of the sum that is paid for driven grouse.

As the popularity of and demand for game-shooting and deer-stalking continued to grow, while the price of wool decreased, sporting lets were developed, and these gradually became more profitable in many Upland areas that had heather and woodland habitats. Many owners used their new-found source of wealth, gained from sporting lets, to invest large sums in the education of their sons at English schools and universities, which was the fashion at the time. This had the effect of breaking the young men's ties with local land stewardship. The lairds' daughters were sent to France or other countries that specialised in finishing schools for young ladies – but very few of them ever got the opportunity to develop and expand their education into worthwhile careers, as this was a strongly male-dominated period. Daughters were for marriage, producing children and, if possible, creating estate amalgamations to add to the wealth of the father, who showed little consideration for the happiness or welfare of the unfortunate girl.

We should also remember the Victorian passion for collecting rare birds and their eggs, which was highly destructive. Similarly, the amassing of plants and ferns for gardens wiped out many of the rarer Upland species. The fashions and excesses of this period, fuelled by finance reaped from the British Empire, were both detrimental and beneficial to the landscapes and habitats which were created, and which changed the face of Scotland.

Two hundred years ago in the Uplands there was a general abundance of wildlife, since the demand did not exceed the natural surplus. Many of the sporting estates established the substantial woodlands of broadleaves and conifers that are now major conservation areas. When Queen Victoria bought Balmoral Estate, she not only began the royal family's love affair with Scotland, which has continued to this day: she also made ownership of upland estates fashionable and popular.

The management of wildlife and countryside took on a new professional meaning, which changed the face of the country. A number of old-established estates like Blair Atholl, Invercauld and Black Mount had been managing wildlife for sport for many years, but it was the interest and the publicity from Balmoral which made it the 'in thing' to do. The change came at a time when sheep were less profitable and the demand for wool was being satisfied by the use of fast ships from Australia and New Zealand. The cargoes were probably being produced by the sons and daughters of immigrants who had been forced to go Down Under from Scotland as a result of the expansion of sheep husbandry 100 years or so previously, so we can see a little justice in this irony.

Soon the wealth of the industrial south began moving north to develop old estates and build new ones, with shooting lodges, houses, roads and bridges, and thus a new prosperity returned to the hills and glens. As the demand for sport escalated, the natural, harvestable surpluses had to be increased by managing the habitat and the quarry species in a way that gave them the best possible conditions. These artificially high surpluses were partly achieved by killing any creature considered detrimental to game species.

In some glens another Upland clearance took place, as crofters were moved to make way for red deer. The herds were now managed, with females being virtually protected and many woods planted as sanctuaries for their increasing population. Large areas of heather moorland were managed for red grouse, and any bird or animal seen as a threat to them was eliminated.

Rivers were developed and managed for game fish, especially salmon. Large numbers of men were employed, and as the years went by great expertise in the management of game was achieved. The development of better guns and rifles greatly improved the standard of shooting until it became a fine art.

It was shooting of a different kind that heralded a change in society and in the countryside, from which neither would never fully recover. The machine-gun slaughter of the innocents in the First World War was followed, in 1939 by the Second World War, which could at least be justified on the grounds that it was a fight for freedom.

It was nevertheless the catastrophic effects of the two World Wars which devastated large numbers of estate owners, stalkers and gamekeepers and the habitats they managed. The loss of the financial base and much management expertise caused a deterioration in the state of the countryside which has eventually resulted in the wretched situation which now exists throughout Britain. Politically-motivated, short-term grant aid, and knee-jerk reactions in response to pressure groups and spin doctors, whose agenda has nothing to do with long-term conservation or land stewardship, do not produce good habitat. An environment managed without informed skills will not save our endangered species or maintain the wealth of wildlife found within our sporting estates.

My Grandfather David ("Dancie") Rose.

Chapter 2

THE VICTORIAN ROMANCE WITH THE HIGHLANDS

MY grandfather David Rose began service with the royal family on Balmoral estate during the second half of the reign of Queen Victoria, when he was appointed as a deer stalker and settled in an estate house called Knock Cottage. He was a famous highland dancing instructor, who taught in many of the Deeside villages. He instructed most of the Royal family at dancing classes held at Balmoral Castle, and his ability to dance while playing the violin earned him the nickname 'Dancie Rose'.

To understand people's excitement about travelling to Scotland, and their commitment to participating in all the forms of Highland recreation during that period, involves some insight into contemporary attitudes. The Victorian and to some extent the Edwardian way of life at home was limited by severe restrictions on what we today regard as natural human behaviour. Emotional exhibitions of love, joy, sadness, togetherness and happiness were all seen as signs of weakness. Class distinction of the upstairs/downstairs type only reinforced this suppression of emotion, and rendered the daily lives of the gentry very stilted. The lives of the royal family were the most restricted of all.

It was only natural that to be released from this stuffy strait-jacket for a few months each year was in itself a huge pleasure and relief. When the royal family travelled north to Balmoral and into the remoteness of the Scottish hills, they could rejoice in the freedom, and the friendliness and affection of the estate staff, and take the opportunity to relax, release their innermost feelings and enjoy themselves uninhibitedly. To them, the sporting Highlands represented a wonderland.

By this time – the 1850s – the shooting etiquette and organisation of large Upland estates had been developed to a high standard, and the professional expertise of the estate staff created a general abundance of wildlife. It is worth considering some of the duties and customs of the estate workers of this period, since we all owe so much to the hard work and professional dedication of men like my grandfather, whose understanding of and bond with wildlife have never been surpassed, despite all the recent advances in technology. Their practical experience of fish, birds or deer, and their understanding of their habitats, made them excellent wildlife managers.

All large Upland estates at that time were run as holiday homes, and had to cater for a variety of tastes. Balmoral, in particular, received not only large numbers of visiting British VIPs such as the Prime Minister, the Archbishop of Canterbury and so on, but also kings and queens from all over the world. Queen Victoria's love for all things Scottish meant that the local people were very much involved in all aspects of the entertainment provided for the royal family's guests. There was great demand for Highland dancing, so my grandfather would quite often go to the castle to dance after a full day of walking on the hill. He also had the honour of acting as Master of Ceremonies for estate balls held for the royal family and their guests. Several of the other Balmoral deer stalkers were accomplished pipers.

In 1901 King Edward VII appointed my father (also called David) as personal stalker to the Prince of Wales, and they became good friends. When the prince came to the throne as King George V in 1910, he presented my father with a telescope and stalking knife which are still in my possession. It was a great personal honour for me to return to Balmoral as a guest of the present Prince of Wales in 1982, and to use this same knife on an old stag I was invited to cull on very same ground where it had been used by my father. King George V was recognised as one of the finest shotgun shots of his generation, and my father always acted as his loader in Scotland, which was part of his duties as the king's personal ghillie.

Much time and effort went into arranging outdoor picnics. Capacious hampers were taken on horseback to distant hilltops, and their exotic contents were enjoyed by large numbers of guests. On the way home they would sometimes stop at a pre-arranged point on a loch-side, where the wildlife staff would row out in a boat with a net to catch some trout. These were then cooked and eaten on the spot as the sun began to set, and a favourite picnic site was an old shooting lodge that the Queen particularly liked to use, by the side of Loch Muick.

My grandfather often referred to one of those picnics, when he was looking after Queen Alexandra, Queen Mary and the Dowager Empress of Russia, and he spent some time rowing them across the loch in a small boat. In later years he was often heard to remark, 'I wonder what would have happened if the boat had sunk that day?'

I am certain it was their memories of holidays like that which gave the royal family their enduring love and affection for Scotland. Balmoral still offers our royal family great joy and contentment, despite the fact that so much of the freedom and privacy enjoyed by Queen Victoria and her successors has been lost because of the need for tight security and the deplorably intrusive and ill-mannered behaviour of a minority of the press.

Tragedy struck our family in 1925, when my grandfather was drowned in the River Dee. Nobody knew exactly what happened, but it seems that he was making his way home across the river after dark and was blown off his feet by a fierce gale, striking his head against a rock. His body was found four days later.

He was much mourned at Balmoral and in the district around – but life had to go on. The popularity of the sporting land-use pioneered by the Victorians brought tremendous prosperity to the country and its people. Those who do not understand man's natural wish to shoot and fish should be aware that it is only as a result of this desire that thousands of trees were planted to enhance the landscape and shelter the wildlife around the estate residences. It was Queen Victoria who personally saved one of the most beautiful and important Caledonian pine woods, called Ballochbuie, from being cut down.

Each estate employed a large staff. There would be a factor or agent, a head stalker and at least one stalker for each beat, together with gamekeepers, fishing ghillies, foresters, gardeners, road-men, builders, carpenters and a complete staff to run the castle or shooting lodge and look after all the domestic and sporting requirements of the owner and his guests.

A home farm would provide fresh food such as butter, vegetables, meat and so on. In the local village there would be at least one minister, policeman, doctor, cobbler, food supplier and taxidermist. From this list it is clear how important sport was and still is in many rural areas. We can also add to the list the establishment of local hotels and the employment of staff to run them.

My father and I often discussed the various sporting activities that he and the other members of the wildlife management staff were required to provide for the guests who stayed at Balmoral during the year. Those pursuits were also provided on other estates throughout Scotland, and are still available to this day, making a major contribution to conservation which is well understood by those who participate in field sports.

When many countryside and conservation issues are so badly misunderstood by the public, perhaps I should refer to some of them, in the hope that by understanding the habitat-management required to provide the food-chains to maintain quarry species, and the wildlife-management needed to provide and sustain an annual surplus, people will realise that this can only be achieved by the application of effective and practical conservation policies and pest control.

It is during the winter months that the wildlife staff lay the foundations that are so important for the long-term environmental welfare of any estate, and Balmoral was no exception. When the guests reluctantly left for the south to resume their duties in many parts of the world, my father would be there with the other stalkers and gamekeepers to form a wildlife-management team under the direction of the factor and the head stalker.

The first priority would be to control the red deer herd by selectively reducing the total breeding population through the annual cull of hinds (females). Sick or injured stags were also removed at this time.

All the stalkers and keepers were experienced with both rifle and shotgun, and they had to carry out necessary forest protection in young plantations of regenerating pine by removing rabbits and hares in large numbers. This often would entail the shooting of thousands of mountain hares, which was necessary to permit the regeneration of heather, grass and blaeberry that would provide essential food and cover for black grouse and capercaillie.

As the forests were mainly of Scots pine and birch, protective fences could eventually be removed when the trees were well established, giving the deer shelter. Hill roads and pony paths were repaired. Weather permitting, the team would repeatedly return to the hills and moors to carry out organised heather burning. Throughout this important period of winter work each stalker was responsible for strict pest control on his particular beat. During bad weather the deer were fed supplementary food in the form of hay, turnips, potatoes and beans.

Each new sporting season started when the melting snows of spring would herald the first runs of salmon that would rush up the rising waters of the River Dee, providing fishing of the finest quality for those early guests to the castle who were skilled with rod and line. Although bait fishing was permitted at times of high flood water, fly-fishing with an eighteen-foot greenheart rod, balanced with a large brass reel, and using the specialised Spey casting technique, was the preferred option. Many members of the royal family have been noted for their skill as fly-fishers, and my family connections permit me to state that at the top of this list we can put Queen Elizabeth the Queen Mother, who was for most of her long life regarded as a fly-fisher of the highest order.

With the warmer weather of late spring, the guests could extend their fishing from the river to mountain burns and lochs and finally, in the early summer when the snows had retreated to the high corries and mountain tops, their challenge was the wily old brown trout that lived in the crystal water of Lochnagar – water so clear that the slightest error with fly or line meant that nothing would be caught.

Yet the fishers who climbed to this mountain loch were never disappointed, because they spent a few magical hours in a remote and isolated place. Wild solitude and space for meditation are priceless assets that lie hidden in many parts of the Scottish Highlands, and can be found by those who know and appreciate them. The quarry is only a bonus: it is the experience and memories that really count. August the Twelfth would herald the start of the game-bird season. The red grouse would be pursued by small parties of guns who would walk the heather hills supported and guided by the local staff. The keepers and handlers would work their highly-trained dogs – pointers and setters that would find the grouse and stand rock-still, noses trained on the spot where the birds lay in hiding. The quarry would be flushed by the dog on command at the appropriate time – always a moment of truth for sporting guests: as the pointer remains rigid and the birds do not rise, time seems to stand still, and the Gun struggles in vain to control emotions that can only be understood and appreciated by those who have participated.

The build-up to this moment would have begun some time previously – the expectation during the journey north, the arrival at the estate with its countless memories, the hills, the forests, the purple heather in all its glory, the annual reunion of friends with guests and estate staff, the renewal of acquaintances at the gun-room in the morning and of that special relationship between stalker and guest as they shake hands, re-forming a bond that outsiders will never understand.

All this must be put aside at the critical moment, when concentration and expectation must unite as the dog flushes the grouse, the birds taking flight just as they would when disturbed by any other predator. There is a sudden flutter of wings and feathers, accompanied by alarm calls from the covey as they take off. The sporting guest nearest to the dog must identify the appropriate bird and swing his gun through its flight-line with an uninterrupted movement, firing at where the bird is going and not at where it is, if the shot is to be successful. As with all predator-prey contacts, the prey will successfully avoid death in the majority of instances, and all field sports should seek to ensure that this is the case.

In areas where red grouse were found in higher densities, they were driven towards the guns. A combination of fair weather, stiff breezes and skilful manipulation of the drive by the keepers' team could produce the finest game shooting in the world, sometimes further enhanced on the higher hilltops by the occasional ptarmigan hurtling from one rocky mountain ridge to another.

As the first russet shades of autumn tinted the trees and grasses, and the crispness of the cold, early-morning air prompted the red deer stags to prepare for the rut, game-shooting took place on lower slopes where black grouse and capercaillie were driven at tree-top height around pine-covered contours, providing high, fast snap-shots that tested the abilities of even the most experienced and talented marksmen.

Balmoral was and still is primarily a red deer forest, but during the many years my family worked there a wide variety of sporting activity was maintained by the royal family. This was made possible only by leasing more ground from the adjoining estates of Birkhall, Abergeldie and Invercauld.

The professional deer stalker's priority is to ensure that visitors are capable of making a humane kill, and that they are fit enough to walk several miles over steep and rough terrain. If a client reveals that he is inexperienced, the stalker will do his utmost to ensure he has safe and enjoyable days on the hill. I have been in this position on several thousand occasions, and consider it a privilege to have shared such moments.

Shooting ability can be ascertained on the range, firing at a target, but when an experienced stalker meets a guest for the first time, he makes several mental notes. My father taught me to understand that new tweeds, new rifle and new boots usually meant trouble on the hill. In those days hill boots were usually made from thick leather which required several coatings of oil and some running-in before they were worn in earnest. When I was responsible for somebody unenlightened, I would ask him to sit with his feet in a pool of water while I spied for the deer. Perhaps he thought it was some strange Scottish ritual, but my concern was to soften the leather of his boots, so that he got off the hill without too many blisters!

Naturally, it was when the stags were rutting that Balmoral was at the height of its sporting year. Red deer stalking over hill terrain is a specialised sport that has been developed into a fine art, and offers an unequalled recreational opportunity to those who are physically fit.

Many of the royal family were experienced and capable deer stalkers in their own right. But protocol demanded they always had their personal stalker with them, and very close friendships were formed between stalker and royal sportsman. Consequently, just as King George V preferred to have my grandfather with him on the hill, my father had the same relationship with Edward, Prince of Wales.

It is perhaps true to say that the stalkers at Balmoral had a tougher and more challenging time than those on most other Highland estates, because many of the visiting VIPs were more accustomed to the City of London and to politics than to the mountainous splendour of Aberdeenshire. Yet the estate staff were, on the whole, much better off than their social equals working in the coal mines and mills of the south. The wildlife staff were the elite, with their own specially-patterned tweed suits or kilts to distinguish them from other servants, and to encourage loyalty and pride in their individual estates.

The head stalkers were men of importance, and commanded great respect in the community. The owner and his guests would have been foolish indeed not to be fully aware that the head stalker was like a general in charge of his troops. The success or failure of a stalking expedition was heavily dependent on this man, so a deep understanding and mutual respect developed between the stalker and the owner, and often spanned many generations.

Many of the Highland deer stalkers were quite forthright and down-to-earth with their opinions. As a result, their views were highly valued by some members of the royal family, who were well aware that the people surrounding them usually gave answers which they thought royalty wished to hear, or were politically correct. The blunt opinions of those who lived close to the soil, with all the wisdom which comes from that association, have been valued by a many owners and employers. A good example of this was Queen Victoria's great faith in the opinions of John Brown, and I am sure that such friendships have been of value to many members of the royal family, both past and present. King George V was so close to my father that he habitually addressed him as 'David' – a form of familiarity which greatly

Queen Elizabeth the Queen Mother presenting the author with the Churchill Fellowship Award.

annoyed less favoured members of the royal staff.

My own friendship with Prince Charles goes back over some 30 years. During that time we have worked with others on matters of conservation and wildlife management. The Prince is held in the highest regard by those who care for the countryside, and I am certain that, if he had not been born to be king, he would have made an excellent wildlife manager. His respect for nature is shared by all those who chose this vocational way of life.

Highland estate ownership is often misunderstood by those who do not know how the countryside works. Fortunately, the royal family, through generations of experience at Balmoral, understand and appreciate this recreational form of land-use.

One of the most important assets of a Highland estate is its solitude, and the wise owner is well aware of the potent effect of this. The mountains and their relationship with mother earth can provide the perfect setting for close relationships not always possible on a driven game day with a party of ten guns, however happy and enjoyable that may be.

Many a major obstacle or diplomatic problem has been talked over and resolved in the tranquillity of an isolated hillside. Coming as I do from three generations of professional deer stalkers, and imbued with our code of silence and confidentiality on such matters, I cannot illustrate this with specific examples; but I can say that kings, queens, nobility and commoners have all experienced this bond.

The owners of Highland properties are fortunate if they can be run as financially viable units, but this is seldom achievable, and substantial investment is normally needed. Luckily those who understand the countryside, and who wish to commune with nature, see the estates as priceless assets that can be shared with numerous others who have similar respect for and understanding of the vital contribution they make to conservation.

Balmoral stalkers, home beat: David Rose, Donald McHardy, Frank Gordon, Jim Torry, Ronnie McGregor, Hamish Abercrombie.

Chapter 3

THE END OF AN ERA

BY the early part of the 20th century the number of estates being developed for sport had reached its climax. The demand for shooting and fishing was still on the increase, however, and the land-owners responded by diversifying their habitats and also developing artificial means of incubation for pheasants and partridges.

Firearms improvements had already led to the perfection of hammerless ejector sporting shotguns. Made to fit the client and to suit his precise requirements, they were often produced in sets of two or three identical weapons. The sportsman could enlist the help of a loader who would stand beside him at the drive, loading and changing his guns quickly, and so allowing him to shoot at more birds in quick succession. Many record bags were shot in this way in this era, aided by the expertise of numerous gamekeepers who maintained large populations of game birds.

With the almost professional attitude of some of the premier shooting men of this period, the standard of shooting was of the highest order. I remember my father telling me about one royal gentleman he used to load for who, on a driven-grouse day at Balmoral, would often kill 99 per cent of the birds he shot at. His guns would get so hot that he would shoot wearing pigskin gloves to protect his hands.

Rifles for shooting deer had become progressively more accurate and reliable, with excellent repeating bolt actions and magazines that could hold 3 to 5 rounds of ammunition. They were only half the weight or less of the old, double-barrelled rifles that had been so common in the early days of stalking.

Fishing was also very popular. There were two main types of game fishing rod, made from split cane or greenheart. Long greenheart rods in particular were used on the large salmon rivers. They were kept in balance by a heavy brass reel, and skilful fishing with them was a fine art.

I often watched my father practice on the lawn at the start of the season, to obtain the correct balance for his rod. He used a special technique known as the 'Spey cast' that was capable of taking the fly far out over the water. It was made by waving the rod back and forth so that three long twists of line would form, suspended in the air. Then, with one final forward flick of the rod, the fly would travel far over the river and land right in front of where the fish were lying.

While practising, my father could take the top off a daisy at the far end of our lawn, such was his accuracy, gained from many happy years of fishing on the River Dee. I was never able to cast like that.

By the 1900s many of the estates had been in operation for several generations, and a high degree of expertise had been accumulated, along with special attention to sporting etiquette. Most properties were still managed by factors, who were responsible for the day-to-day running. They lived on the estates and their job was to look after the interests of the owner. Fishing, shooting, farming and forestry were managed together in harmony, to the benefit of all four.

The outbreak of the First World War heralded another change to the Uplands. Thousands of the key men who were responsible for the daily running of the estates were sent to France, where their expertise with a rifle and in fieldcraft meant that many of them were put into special units in the front line. Many became snipers.

A high proportion of them would never see their beloved hills again, and they were greatly missed. My father was one of those who left Balmoral to join the family regiment, the Gordon Highlanders.

At that time it was the practice in the army to put all the men from one area into the same platoon so that they would know each other. This was a great error of judgement, because a single battlefield engagement could wipe out the whole unit, with great heartbreak, hardship and loss to one or more villages.

Many years later, when I myself had become a soldier in the Gordon Highlanders, I was on a recruiting tour in Aberdeenshire. We stopped at a remote war memorial to play 'The Flowers of the Forest' on the bagpipes as a mark of respect to the soldiers who had lost their lives in the Battle of the Somme in 1916, where 95 per cent of young men from the vicinity had been killed. As I stood to attention and ran my eyes down the lists of several hundred names, I felt that I could relate to many of them.

I had been fortunate in being brought up in a valley similar to theirs and, like them, I too had been nurtured in the love, trust and freedom of an extended family. I had the freedom to fish in the burn, watch the deer and hear the grouse call in the heather. I attended the village school in all its protective isolation, and then at fourteen years of age I went to work on the estate with people whom I already knew and respected in the community.

Other young men were not so fortunate as they travelled to Aberdeen for the first time, a train journey followed by a boat journey to France. This was all very exciting for brave but also naive youngsters, and many ended their short lives with their faces in the mud of France. I wonder if their last thoughts were of home and the glen, and the loved ones they would never see again, or of the wind in their hair or the rain on their faces.

Did they wonder how it all happened so fast, and about the senseless stupidity of it all? Perhaps if those who started the war had been the first to go over the edge of the trench into a hail of bullets, wiser counsels would have prevailed. I was destined to be a soldier for a few more years, and such is the innocence of youth that you always think that it will never happen to you. Alas, all too often, it did happen.

My father was one of the fortunate ones to return from the First World War. He was wounded twice, but lived to tell the tale. As far as the Rose family were concerned, the only good thing to come out of this whole sorry affair was the arrival of my mother. After the Battle of the Somme, my father met Jeanne Julienne Louise Faes. They were married in France, and returned to Balmoral, where he was again employed as a deer-stalker to King George V.

In 1918 the country rejoiced at the peace, thinking that this would be the last war. The fortunate ones returned to pick up where they had left off, but life could never be the same. Many of the estate owners had been killed, and their sons also, leaving some distant relative as an unexpected heir, often with new ideas. Some understood stewardship of the land and worked to maintain it, while others took without giving. Much land was soon up for sale and divided into smaller areas. Other individuals simply lost their estates at the gambling tables.

The 1920s and 1930s brought change to the countryside as it recovered from the ravages of the war, which had left many rural areas robbed of their youth. Some men did return to the tranquil surroundings of their glens, but remained psychologically changed for the rest of their lives. Restlessness and the attractions of the city would cause a proportion of them to forsake the tranquillity of the hills.

After the First World War the Government was principally concerned with the problems of towns and cities. The soldiers returning home with high hopes of prosperity and a better life had their expectations dashed on the rocks of reality, as there was simply no work for them. They were not prepared to exchange the trenches of France for the dole queues of Britain. They rioted in the streets and marched to London to demand employment.

As a result, financial support was gradually deployed in coal-mining, ship-building, car and textile manufacture and other related industries. The countryside was left to fend for itself, and town and countryside were treated as separate entities. The main reasons for this were working conditions and lack of transport. The average working week was six days, and only the privileged few had cars.

Holidays were an annual event, taken when the factories and mines closed down for a set period, and the majority of the work-force took a train or bus to the seaside. Bicycles were a common form of transport but tended to be used only for local travel and as a necessary means of getting to work.

Land-values over most of the Uplands were low, and properties were cheap to purchase. Those with the money to invest in hill farming or sport on estates were able to acquire very large areas, compared with the average acreage of a lowland farm on richer ground.

As industries in the populated areas began to prosper, creating wealth for those in the fortunate position of owning or managing them, the demand for shooting and fishing increased again. The management of wildlife and its habitats was developed once more to accommodate this new transfusion of money.

Tourism was expanding in certain areas such as Loch Lomond and the Trossachs, which had all become well known thanks to the novels of Sir Walter Scott. Tales of a monster in Loch Ness, the royal family's continuing close links with Deeside, and numerous stirring tales and legends such as the massacre of Glencoe all contributed to fire people's enthusiasm for the Scottish Highlands, and helped to bring a much needed cash flow into the north.

We need to be aware that most of the major changes that take place on our land come as a result of Government policies made far away from the countryside that will be affected by them. They are generally made by people who, with little or no practical experience of front-line wildlife and forestry management, are prompted by short-term problems or political motivation.

It was unfortunate that, as the demands on the countryside increased, Government subsidies towards the land were aimed at stimulating food production and the expansion of softwood afforestation, at the expense of the many other natural habitats that are vital for the long-term welfare of wildlife. It was not appreciated that professional wildlife management would be essential for the welfare of the countryside as a whole. This is now all too obvious to all of us who work in the countryside at the dawn of the 21st century. I hope, for the sake of our grandchildren, that the diligent land stewardship of past generations will be encouraged to return.

This will be a major responsibility for the recently-devolved Scottish Parliament. I can only hope that its members will learn from past mistakes and consult the full-time professionals who work daily with farming, forestry and field sports, when they are formulating long-term policies for the management of wildlife and the countryside.

MY CHILDHOOD

Chapter 4

FLOOD, FISH AND FOAMING RIVER

MY first glimpses of the wonders of the natural world were got from my father's back as he carried me around the Balmoral estate on his bicycle, in his game bag, even though I was too young to remember those lovely surroundings or the royal owners who took such a personal interest in their estate staff and families.

I was born in the West Lodge, near the castle, and Queen Mary attended my christening in Crathie Church. It was the custom of a number of the royal family to call in for a chat when out for a walk, and as my French-born mother could not speak much English at the time, members of the royal household would visit her and talk to her in French.

It was during such a visit that King George V was having a cup of tea with my mother, and I was sitting on the living room floor. The king observed me digging out the earth from between the flagstones with my fingers and remarked, 'This is not good for the boy. I'll see the factor about a new floor'. This was promptly installed and remained in use by successive stalkers and their families until recently, when the whole cottage was renovated by the present Queen.

I have a dog whistle and chain that I wear on my waistcoat, and one of the medals on the chain reads:

'For Long and Faithful Service – D. Rose From G.R.V.'.

It represents my father's 30 years at Balmoral.

In 1939, when I was 3 years old, the Forestry Commission built four small-holdings in the hills midway between Loch Lomond and the Trossachs in Central Scotland, an area now known as the Queen Elizabeth Forest Park. They were called the Corrie Holdings and the first to be completed in March of that year was intended for a 'forest trapper', or 'forest ranger' as they are now called.

My father moved south from Balmoral to take up his new appointment, and so began another chapter in the life of the Rose family, who for the next 32 years were all employed in the management of forests and the wildlife associated with them. Even though we had shifted our ground, I was able to keep up my contact with Deeside, as several other members of my family worked for the Queen Mother.

My childhood in the Corrie Holdings provided me with a priceless practical understanding of the wildlife and habitats of the Uplands, and of man's place in nature. I was the youngest of a family of five, with one sister and three brothers, and we were surrounded by people who lived on the land, with fishing, shooting, farming and forestry being the principal employment.

Two of the four new crofts of our little community had been designed for keeping cattle, and two for poultry. Our other immediate neighbours were one large hill-farm and another small croft. With the exception of the farm manager, everybody worked for the Forestry Commission. This included my sister and any of the other wives who wished to have a job.

As I spent most of my time with my father, my older brothers and the other wildlife staff, I was in a good position to learn the ways of the countryside. Happy memories of sledging in the snow, white, crisp and spotless in the absence of pollution, and the rippling of the trout stream in the cold clear air, remain vivid reminders of the winter scene. Spring time meant the cries of the golden plover, lapwings and skylark as they nested in their hundreds, free from excessive predation and the dangers of modern agriculture.

Memories of running barefoot in summer after a shower of rain, with the rich and evocative smell of bog myrtle all around, will stay with me forever. Late summer resounded with the cry of the red grouse, and then in autumn the roaring of the red deer stags would herald the coming of winter.

I was part of it all, far from the madding crowd, childishly unaware that outside this small world of mine a madman called Hitler was starting a world war that would affect my family and all who lived near us. My father and my three brothers prepared for to fight, while I remained with the local wildlife, carefree and blissfully oblivious of the danger.

The small stream that ran past our house held a special attraction for me as a boy of five. When the water was low in the summer I spent many happy hours searching under the overhanging sides of the deeper pools and flat stones for the lovely little brown trout that hid there. I learned how to identify their exact position by touch, and I knew from experience that they always faced upstream. Once I had located one, I would rub it gently with the tips of my fingers and gradually move my hand forward to its head. Then I would grasp the fish quite firmly between my thumb and fore finger in the gills, and lift it out onto the bank. The local name for this sport was 'guddling', and it gave me countless hours of fun.

Fishing with rod and line soon replaced guddling. I got to know each small burn in detail, so that when the rain came and the river was in flood, I could put my knowledge to good use. There was no carbon fibre in those days, and men would use a split-cane or greenheart fishing rod, but boys of my age would simply cut a hazel sapling from the river bank. Then we would tie on a piece of brown line and a bait hook, dig a few worms from a cow-pat or a caterpillar from the roots of a dock plant, and a-fishing we would go. We knew where the quarry would lie and wait for food, so we could place the bait in exactly the right spot and let it drift downstream towards the fish. We had a great advantage over the visiting fishermen with their expensive equipment but sparse local knowledge of the river and its inhabitants.

Many a sixpence I was paid for my catches by a visitor from Glasgow who wanted to impress his wife and children on his return from his day in the hills. As we grew older, we learned from our elders how to make trout flies similar in size and colour to the insects we observed on the river bank. We would use them on the larger pools of the river and lochs to catch the really big fish.

I remember in particular the Lime Hill Loch, a few miles' walk from our house, that had been stocked by the Duke of Montrose with beautiful Loch Leven trout. Those fish were covered with large black spots, their flesh was pink, and they were especially delicious to eat.

Easter would herald the start of our brown trout season, when the rise in the early morning temperature warmed the rocks where bright, clear mountain streams sparkled and chattered as they rushed off the hillsides at the start of their long journey to the sea via the River Forth.

I would look to the hills with rising excitement and anticipation as the mild south-westerly wind blew the dark, rain-laden clouds onto the steep slopes of Ben Lomond. The rain would fall and the stream would rise, tempting the larger fish to stir from their hidden depths. The rushing flood of water and the promise of abundant food upstream would tempt them to swim for the upper reaches of the small streams that tumbled from the hills around our homestead.

There would be a limited period when fish, flood and food would reach a peak of harmony. I had to be in the right place at the appropriate time to take full advantage of my local knowledge. The first decision was to choose the best stream for the day, based on the size of the pools, the height of the flood water and the local weather, because these were the most important factors that would influence the behaviour of the big fish which would swim upstream for the day to feed.

Off I would set through squelching bog with my faithful companion, my labrador dog. On our journey we would often be overtaken by the resident heron as it flew overhead in the direction of our destination, so we were certain that the fish would be there. That bird knew more about fish and the art of catching them than I would ever learn, as his survival depended on it.

On my arrival at the chosen burn in some remote valley, I would read the water like a map. First, a cautious approach to the top of the pool with its patch of white foam highlighting the current in a circular motion, and pin-pointing the place where the local fish would lie. This would be the second place I would try, as the passing fish preferred to lie near the cover of the stream-side willows and the overhanging bank which would occasionally provide the extra advantage of food in the form of caterpillars and insects. The reduction of the speed of the water at this point also allowed them to feast on the food that was being washed downstream in the flood.

I would cast upstream to catch the current that would take my hook past this point, controlling its flow and depth on a loose line and with a sensitive finger so that the bait would pass the fish at a natural speed. Then would come a breathless pause, and a keenly-anticipated pull on my finger which would indicate that a big fish had been outwitted and tempted – a time to control the surge of excitement. Then the second tug, and it was time to tighten the line and strike, all in one priceless moment. The fish wriggled and jumped as a prelude to its rush upstream. The tension on rod and line – vital to eventual success – had to be maintained despite bated breath and fast-beating heart. Patience and skill were rewarded when the flash of the white under-belly indicated that the fish was tiring and might be landed – all part of the natural interplay of predator and prey.

If I was fortunate enough to land a few trout, I would share them with my neighbours, as this was our custom. With a few wild mushrooms gathered on the way home and our fresh fish fried in locally-produced butter, accompanied by potatoes dug from our garden, we would have a meal worthy of the term 'wild harvest'.

When I was a child, our year was governed by the seasons. For us who lived on the upper reaches of the River Forth in Rob Roy country, the salmon arrived in autumn. I can clearly remember my first encounter with this wonderful fish. I was playing in a large tree that overhung the river and looked down into the water below. There in the shadow at the centre of the pool lay the largest fish I had ever seen.

With growing excitement I pondered how to catch it. Near the bank I could see a small island of leaves and branches. If I could drop off the tree onto this place, I might be near enough to get hold of the monster by the tail and pull it to the bank. My concentration on the salmon was so intense that I failed to notice that my little island had two dorsal fins sticking up through the camouflage of leaves. When I dropped onto it there was a sudden splash as my stepping-stone of two other salmon took off upstream, sending me head over heels into the cold water! A little later and much wiser, I set off for home, never dreaming that in the course of time salmon would cast me in the mould of fisherman, poacher and water bailiff, and give me countless memories of frustration, exhilaration, sorrow and joy.

Those first brushes with salmon were brought back to me some forty years later when I was teaching the young son of one of the owners of an estate I was managing. We were looking at the wildlife of upland streams, and came upon a number of salmon which had recently arrived from the River Tweed to spawn. I explained at length why they were there, and said that the boy must not be tempted to touch them as they were now out of season. The look in his eyes and expression on his face brought back memories of my own childhood, and I decided my warning had fallen on deaf ears.

That evening I had cause to visit the boy's house to make arrangements for the next day. Both he and his father were absent, and I was invited in by a very nervous mother whom I had only met on a few occasions before. She appeared to me to be behaving strangely in her kitchen as she prepared a customary cup of tea: this normally bright, kind and sophisticated woman seemed to be having problems with her washing machine.

Next day I received the explanation from an embarrassed father. The young son, unable to resist the temptation, had returned to the stream after my departure. He had successfully landed a salmon by running it onto the small stones at the shallow end of the pool – a fish so large that he had had great difficulty pulling it back to the house.

He had arrived a few minutes before my unexpected visit. His mother, panic-stricken by the presentation of this unexpected prize, sent the boy to his room and put the salmon into the washing machine just as I came to the door. Her greatest fear was that I would see the fish through the machine's window, and so she persistently hovered in front of it while I was having my tea.

Hearing about the fish next day, I insisted that they should all have it for supper, and when the mother got to know me better, we had many more humorous encounters as she slowly learned the real joys of living in the countryside – particularly the truth that on some occasions 'out of season' did not necessarily mean 'off the menu'. On that first occasion one boy's capture of a salmon for the pot was a world away from the activities of a criminal who steals on a large scale and poisons our rivers in the pursuit of greed.

Chapter 5

SHOOTING, SAFETY, GUNS AND GAME

THERE is a time and place for everything, and success comes from experience and practice. With shooting, I was a fortunate beginner, because I had grown up surrounded with firearms. Just as the art of fishing and the knowledge of fish and water were for me a never-ending process, firearms and shooting animals and birds, and getting to know the habitats in which they lived, became a gradual part of my education.

My brothers were also part of this world of shooting, and I had the ideal training as a young boy because I was always with them. Only occasionally did the fact that there was a war on enter my awareness.

At this time my father was a training sergeant with the Home Guard, where his experiences in the Great War were put to good use. My oldest brother Dave was already off to fight with the famous 51st Highland Division, and I only saw him when he was at home on leave. My next brother Jack was working in the forest with my father. Later he became a major influence in my life, but at this time, like so many others of his age, he was called to war, trained, sent abroad, and was badly wounded on his eighteenth birthday in France. He lost a leg and was hit in his chest by shrapnel that could not be moved and remained with him for the rest of his life.

My sister Jean also worked in the forest, and my youngest brother George was a sergeant in the local army cadet unit. Later he became a regimental sergeant-major in the Gordon Highlanders.

War or no war, our house was completely dominated by shooting, fishing and firearms. The first thing I can remember of the hostilities was standing out on the hillside next to our house in bright moonlight and hearing the tremendous roar of engines as hundreds of German bombers passed overhead. My mother had considerable problems trying to stop my father shooting at them with his .303 rifle, as they appeared to be flying very low.

Then came the thunder of their bombs as they dropped them on Clydebank, outside Glasgow, and the sky lit up with the orange glow from the fires the explosions created. Some time later we saw a German plane coming along the hillside and being shot at by a Spitfire: in their attempt to get away the crew dumped their bombs quite near us, but luckily they did no harm, as they landed in a peat bog. We were told later that the plane had been shot down, although we did not see it.

For the six o'clock news, we all gathered around the battery-operated radio to hear what was happening in the outside world. The battery was a re-chargeable type which lasted a week with limited use. I was permitted to hear fifteen minutes of 'Dick Barton, Special Agent', a weekly radio soap called 'The McFlannels', and the Scottish Dance Music program on a Saturday night. These were our radio highlights of the week.

The bombing of Clydebank added an unexpected richness to my life when, a few days after the German attack, a small boy named Stuart Watson walked into the valley to stay with his aunt on a neighbouring croft. He was a refugee from the city, and as we were of the same age the town boy and the country bumpkin became inseparable friends for a few happy years as we roamed wild on the hills. He was street-wise and I was country-wise, and this proved a wonderful mixture that enriched both our lives.

One of our particular pranks was to catch a few wild birds in a live-trap made from a riddle or soil-sieve, when bird watchers came to the forest. It was a constant joy for us to watch them running over hill and dale in hot pursuit of a common blackbird that we had just released after decorating its plumage with a few drops of paint from the garden shed. They were rare birds indeed, and it gave us endless entertainment watching those ornithological experts searching through their books for the names of those exotic and unknown species.

The first rifle I can remember using was a very old B.S.A. airgun belonging to my brothers. It was completely worn out and very inaccurate, but to me, a six-year-old boy, it was perfect, as I was able to pull the barrel down far enough to cock the mechanism. Then I would push a used match-stick into the chamber, close the barrel and go hunting tigers in the forest. Actually my targets were match boxes and tin cans, but in my imagination they were all big game.

We had a very large hen-house on a steep slope next to our house. It commanded a view similar to that seen from the ramparts of a moated fort, as immediately below the windows of the hut was a duck pond in the centre of the extensive hen run. This was a shooting gallery for all the family and friends. One of the windows had been removed and a bench placed inside to provide an ideal firing point. There must be thousands of .22 bullets in the mud at the bottom of that pond – for we spent many happy hours firing at floating match-boxes or leaves. At every miss there would be a splash in the water, much to the enjoyment of the onlookers. Practice makes perfect, and all my family were eventually marksmen.

My father was a quite brilliant shot, and he would leave us all to practise. When we could hit the cork off the top of a wine bottle and felt we had become experts, along he would come to share in our joy, smile and let us brag a little. Then he would send one of us down to a log beside the pond, where we had to stick two or three unused matches tightly into the top. He would then proceed to light them one by one, each with a single bullet, and so bring us all down to earth with a bump. The day did eventually come when we could all do it, but for me this was several years in the future. I had the use of a very small .22 rifle that fitted me quite well. Every time one of my brothers went target-shooting, I was there, and by the age of seven I became quite efficient at it. I also started to learn about shotguns at this time, and had the use of a lovely .410 double-barrelled hammer gun.

Fortunately, my father was extremely strict with us all about safety and the use of firearms. First, they must never be pointed at anybody at any time, be they empty or loaded. We were all taught that a safety-catch should never be considered trustworthy. No weapons might be loaded in the house, and rifle bolts had to be opened twice, and the rifle pointed in the air and the trigger pulled, on returning from shooting, even though this had been previously done on the hill at the end of the shoot.

All shotguns had to be carried in a manner that ensured that the muzzle was never pointed at anyone. In company they had to be broken open so that everybody could see that they were unloaded. This drill, enforced on us at a young stage, soon became second nature. I still perform it automatically and without a second thought every time I use firearms today. You must treat all firearms with respect, as familiarity and complacency can and do kill.

I soon graduated from shooting at tin cans to hunting rats and rabbits with my .22 rifle and with a shotgun. First the target was a tin can on a post, then a tin can floating quickly downstream, and later I am afraid it was old gramophone records flung through the air, as they made ideal clay pigeons. Then the final practice was on rabbits running through the grass – all very exciting for a boy who at this age was surrounded by wildlife but was still too young to appreciate it fully.

The year 1946 brought a new beginning for us all, thankful that the war was at last over and we could make a fresh start. The Home Guard was disbanded, so my father had to hand in his sergeant's stripes and return to his full-time duties as a forest ranger. The Forestry Commission had some new ideas. The forest we lived in was to be let for game-bird shooting in the young plantations. There were quite high numbers of red grouse, black grouse, pheasants and snipe. Roe, red and fallow deer, and also wild goats, lived in the surrounding hills, and the unplanted ground above the tree line was let for red deer stalking in the traditional manner.

My father was in charge of all shooting, and the area was to be run much on the lines of a private estate. This provided a wonderful time for me to grow up in, and to learn about tree protection, conservation and deer management, and how they complement each other. At every opportunity I was out on the hills with the wildlife staff, armed with a walking stick rather than a rifle, as my main duties were to drive the deer out of the trees and other areas where they lay in hiding and move them towards places where they could be ambushed by the riflemen. My most valuable experience came from sitting on a vantage-point on one hill and watching the movements of the professionals stalking deer on the hill opposite. It was these observations that provided me with vital insights into deer and their reactions to stalkers, and a practical understanding that I still use to this day.

My first shooting records tell me that my target practice had paid off, as there is an extensive list of rats, rabbits, hares and so on that I bagged. I was still young, and to be honest I cannot really remember any of them, although I am certain they felt like major triumphs at the time.

One outing I do remember. On the side of a small hill of stunted heather I worked my dog around in the wind while standing by a burrow and waiting for the return of any rabbit that bolted from cover. That day proved different. The dog pointed into some white grass, stopped and looked at me, and on my command 'Fetch it!', pounced.

There was a flurry of movement and up flew a large greyhen, a female black grouse and a common bird in those days. It lifted into the wind and swung over my head. I pulled back the gun's hammers, just as I had so often done when practising with gramophone records, found the bird in the air, and swung through it to see daylight ahead of it. Without stopping the swing I pressed the trigger. A bang, a tuft of feathers in the air, and there one dead game-bird thumping onto the ground at my back.

This was a proud moment in my early sporting life, although I would never shoot at a greyhen today.

Moving down to the next item on the game list, I find, 'Shot two foxes with one shot'. This great event took place on a Sunday. I woke to find that after a dry week rain was just starting, and it was going to be a day for trout fishing on the small streams near the tops of the hills. Worms were hastily dug and a jam jar filled with bait; my trout bag was on my back; and with rod, line and hook I was off up the hill. By the time I reached the high ground the water was rising and I soon had a number of nice brown trout for supper. The stream where I was fishing was about a metre in width and meandered down the hill past our croft on the hillside far below.

I was pushing my way through the bracken-covered bank when I stopped to look ahead and to my surprise I could see a rocky outcrop upstream where there were three or four foxes rolling about in play on top of a large flat stone at the side of a waterfall. I looked again to make sure I was not dreaming. Then off I set at full speed down the hill for my father. I got back to the house to find he was away in the village and would not return until it was dark.

I knew where to find the key for the gun cupboard, opened it, and decided I would take the large 12-bore shot gun that he used for foxes instead of my much smaller .410. I also took some of his Alphamax BB cartridges, and off I went back up the stream side.

I approached the stone ledge with great caution. I looked along the side of the nearest tree, and there were two foxes sitting on top of the ledge. I could hardly breathe with excitement. The area round them was strewn with bits of sheep and lambs and the remains of numerous game-birds, and I suddenly realised that this was the den for which my father had been searching for some time.

I can remember getting two of the cartridges from my pocket, quietly opening the gun, slipping them into the breech and closing it without a sound. When I put the gun up to my shoulder I could not hold it and aim properly, as the butt was far too long for me and I could not reach the trigger. The enthusiasm of youth soon overcame such problems. I stalked slowly forwards to a small tree and managed to rest the barrels on top of it. Grasping the gun firmly, I could look along the rib and see the two foxes sitting up and staring at me about 25 metres away: one inexperienced young boy facing two inexperienced young foxes. Older, wiser animals would have made off in a flash.

As I looked at them, a sudden doubt entered my mind. I had always observed my father pull the front trigger first, pause, then pull the other trigger. I was not certain I could reach them with my fingers, so I decided to pull both triggers simultaneously and hope for the best. So it was that the hunter levelled the gun, took careful aim, and pulled.

What happened next was a blast of pain and excitement – pain as the gun kicked viciously into my shoulder and knocked me backwards into the water; and excitement as I climbed up the bank, ran over to the rock, shaken and wet but not injured, to see that both the foxes were dead. I promptly tied them together, slung them on my back and headed for home like a Canadian fur trapper.

As I laid my bag out on our washing green for all to see, I was informed by my mother that I would get a right good leathering from my father when he returned, and I had to sit in my room until the punishment could be administered. He duly came back from the village, and, having heard the story, said it would be a long time before I ever killed two foxes at one time again – and in this he was right, as I never repeated the fluke. I also remember that the promised thrashing with the belt never took place; just a stern warning not to touch his guns without his permission. But the tone of his voice betrayed his secret pleasure that another of his sons had come of age and would follow in his footsteps.

To those who are not familiar with this way of life, the shooting of those foxes and my satisfaction and joy may seem a strange response from a young boy, so it is perhaps important to explain it. When you are fortunate enough to be brought up in the heart of the countryside and be part of a family totally committed to wildlife management, involved in it each day, you form a respect for, and understanding of, how all the elements in the countryside fit together.

I had already seen the damage that foxes could do to sheep with their throats pulled out and nursing ewes with their milk vessels eaten off, so that their lambs were unable to feed. On the open hills this meant death. Add to this the killing of ducks, hens and numerous ground-nesting wild birds, and fox-control can be seen as a vital part of conservation.

Unfortunately this important fact is deliberately avoided in most television programmes. They depict this beautiful animal as if it were a harmless benefactor that travels the countryside with a first-aid outfit, looking for sick rabbits, when in fact it is really nothing more than an attractive wild dog.

Foxes have a place in our countryside, but as they live in a habitat that has little or no natural balance, their numbers must be controlled for the benefit of all the other wildlife living there. This is especially so in areas of upland hill farms, where the farmer has to protect his livelihood, and for those of us who are employed to protect rare species of birds and animals.

This is the true meaning of conservation – protecting the eggs and young from excessive predation. Foxes have their important place in general scheme of country life, too, and I have spent countless hours watching them in areas where protection was not necessary, and I was delighted to use my binoculars instead of my rifle.

Another vivid memory is of one of the first red deer I stalked and shot, accompanied by my pal Jimmy McLean, the son of a neighbouring crofter. It was on a hill called the Guallan, near the bonnie banks of Loch Lomond.

My father was having serious trouble that winter with a large herd of red deer which came off the hills to eat the young trees on the lower slopes. I was to be given the chance to show how much I had learned about stalking, and he would follow to keep a watchful eye.

Jimmy and I set off towards High Corrie Cottage, some three miles to the north of our homestead, and we lay at the foot of the hill where we could spy the high tops in an attempt to pinpoint the main herd. I planned our route from this vantage point, aware that the breeze was from the west and the stalk had to be upwind.

We were in luck, as we could see a small herd just at the top side of the fence that ran along the 1,500 foot contour (the top planting height in those days). We knew that the herd would be brought over the fence and down into the new plantation by the leading hind, and where she would go, the rest would follow.

Having tested the crosswind and carefully watched the area below her, she decided it was safe, and set off, unaware of the two mighty hunters a mile below her. We now had to cross into the cleft of a small stream that would hide us while we climbed to a rowan tree that stood opposite a prominent stone on the hillside. The path that the deer had taken came past the stone, and they would reach the spot in about half an hour. By then we would have to be in position. Soon we reached our rowan tree, climbed up the steep banks of the stream and moved over towards the rock that lay some 200 yards to the left. We managed this by crawling along on our hands and knees in the small ditches dug by the forest workers when they had prepared the area for planting some two years before. It was wet and dirty, but we had no other way to approach our position, and we dared not lift our heads, for fear that the leading hind would see us.

Previous experience had taught me that deer spend most of their time looking downhill, and that the best approach is therefore either across the hill towards them or down from above them. Neither of those options was available to us on this occasion, but the drainage ditch made the approach possible. So it was that two very excited, wet and muddy boys reached the stone and could sit up, suitably hidden, and make their final plans.

We slowly edged round the side, and there they were, with the first part of the herd some 100 metres away. They were slowly grazing in our general direction, but we knew we had a problem as they were feeding into the wind, and their advance was likely to take them past in front of our hiding place at a range too great for my small rifle.

As we watched them grazing towards us, enjoying the fresh grass with the occasional young top of a conifer being added to the menu, some of the younger animals would stop and chase each other in circles. These playful antics were pushing the herd towards us, so we might still be in luck. I slowly climbed up the short distance to the top of the rock and pulling myself up by using some tufts of grass growing on its top, I slid forwards to have a grandstand view.

As I lay there, the number of deer in view gradually increased as they all grazed forwards. I could not make up my mind which one would be best for eating – the quality of the venison being of major importance – and I tried to think of all the things my brothers and father had taught me about size, shape, colour, sex, in or out of season and so on. And I was lost.

Then a strange thing happened that froze me to the rock. One of the mature females stopped eating and stared right at me for several minutes. At last she put her head down again, giving me enough time to slip my small rifle onto the tussock of moss that would afford a good rest if I had a chance to shoot. As always with deer that think they have seen something suspicious, they pretend to feed for a moment and then suddenly look back and stare directly at the same spot; but I was safely behind my clump of grass, or so I thought.

As I lay there watching this hind along the barrel, I knew from her reactions that she had seen me. The first indication came from her ears, which stiffened and turned in my direction like radar discs. Her front legs went straight as she pushed her feet down into the grass. Then she carefully lifted one and tapped it on the ground, giving a signal to all the other mature members of the herd that there could be danger. The rest of the deer were alerted, and would immediately react to any decision she made.

I felt sure all was lost, and wondered what my father would have done in this situation. I lay flat on top of my vantage point waiting for the gruff bark from the leading hind that would send the whole lot dashing off up the hill, without question in the direction of Ben Lomond. But it did not happen, and quite slowly the herd began eating again. Perhaps the leader thought that the movement she had seen had been a bird landing on a stone. I lay still, as I knew what would happen next.

The hind pretended to graze for a few seconds, then quite suddenly turned round and held the object of her curiosity in a fixed stare, in the hope of catching the enemy off guard. I just lay safely behind the grass.

Sure enough she again looked up and gazed in my direction. I smiled with satisfaction, having learnt this trick from my father – but my pleasure was short-lived, as the deer started walking slowly but quite deliberately towards me, stopping every few metres to flare her nostrils in an attempt to scent the object of her curiosity.

Fortunately the wind was in my favour and she was soon well within my shooting range, so I slowly cocked my rifle by pulling back the end of the bolt. Thankfully it did not make a sound.

I brought the rifle peep-sight into the aim (we did not have telescopic sights in these days) and, with a major effort, steadied my shaking hands by grasping the barrel tightly and pressing my wrist into the moss. I took a deep breath and, having got a steady aim, fired and killed the unfortunate animal instantly. I had shot my first deer at the age of ten.

What had made the hind walk towards me on this occasion? Quite simply her curiosity (fortunate for me) and her poor eyesight. In those days I was blessed with a thick crop of bright auburn hair, and as I lay on top of the stone it was blowing in the wind. This was enough to interest the deer, but unfortunately for her it did not indicate danger to herself or the herd. How time passes! If the same incident were to happen today, it would be the sun glistening on my bald head that would attract attention.

On that day I learnt another important lesson in red deer stalking – that of 'the long carry home'. I knew how to bleed and clean the animal, and with this duly completed we decided that we must take the whole carcase back so that everyone could share the venison. We were two fit boys, but 120 pounds of meat had to be carried several miles through bog myrtle and heather and over numerous drainage ditches, ensuring that it was two very tired lads who eventually reached the corrie-holding that night.

That long carry home would not be forgotten for the rest of our lives. Little did we know that young Jimmy would return in 1983 as senior harvesting forester, to cut down the young trees we were protecting on that day. I was also to spend most of my life protecting trees from deer, and this was the first of many thousands I would shoot in the name of forest protection.

Chapter 6

FRANCE, PREDATORS AND PRIVILEGE

MY education at this time in my life laid the foundations for a set of standards, ideals and views that developed and sustained me for many years to come. Academically I was a complete failure, and it was not the teachers' fault that I did not make use of the education I received at Balfron High School, although my many happy hours working in the school garden made me aware of the relationship between soil, plants and animals in a way that would have a major influence on my work in years ahead.

Unfortunately, my mind was never in the classroom, as my thoughts seldom left the wildlife at home. My attitude to school is best described by the poet Robert Burns, who wrote:-

My heart's in the Highlands, my heart is not here,
My heart's in the Highlands a-chasing the deer;
A-chasing the red deer and following the roe,
My heart's in the Highlands wherever I go.

My first adventure away from my home village took place when I went with my parents to Hazebrook in France, to see our French relatives. I had never been on a train, so the journey south on the famous Flying Scotsman, with its hissing of steam and columns of black coal smoke and endless clickety-click as we travelled south, provided sights and sounds I would never forget. Then to Dover, and my first sighting of big ships, enormous compared with the rowing boats I had seen on Loch Lomond. Then the sea with its endless waves, and the sound of them lapping to and fro against the white cliffs of Dover. All these things were so new and different from the quiet hills of home. The cries of the numerous seagulls seemed a poor substitute for the calls of golden plover, curlew and grouse.

On to Calais, with its stevedores, the brightly-coloured berets of policemen with firearms at their sides, and a flamboyant race of people who waved their arms while speaking and kissed on both cheeks instead of shaking hands. It was all so different from my friends in the Scottish glens, but all part of the richness of life and a new experience. France was just beginning to recover from the ravages of war, with the pock-marks of shrapnel and bullets clearly visible on the outsides of most of the larger buildings. All the major roads had hastily-repaired craters along them, which showed the amazing accuracy of Allied bombing.

We went to see one of our uncles who had just been presented with one of France's highest gallantry awards for his work with the Resistance. He had welded a special box into the tender of his train engine, and this he used to conceal prisoners of war – mainly RAF crews who had been shot down. As a train driver he had the perfect cover to do this dangerous service for the Allies. Thankfully, he was never caught.

My father visited an old church and was surprised to find its roof still covered by the ivy that had hidden the German sniper who shot him during the First World War. He always had shown a kind of respect for this sniper, as he was a marksman who had been a deer hunter in Germany, so they actually had a lot in common. Father was very fortunate that his opponent specialised in shooting his victims through the ankle, as he was only interested in putting them out of active service and causing maximum logistical problems for the British enemy. Before he was captured, he sent a large number of injured British soldiers home, and in so doing had actually saved many of them from death.

The three main memories I have from that visit were not connected with the war. The first was the toilets, as our cottage had always had hot and cold water and a flush toilet, and I had innocently assumed that everybody had the same. So the French hole in the ground, with its abundance of wildlife growing inside, was an unforgettable novelty. The second memory was connected with my habit of drinking a glass of cold spring water with each meal. This was not possible in France, as they had no fresh drinking water, so I was permitted to drink wine. This made me feel very grown-up, and also light-headed as I would quite often have an extra glass when nobody was looking.

My final memory was quite unexpected, as it was to do with rabbits. At home I had become quite good at shooting rabbits for dinner, so it was a strange feeling and something difficult to come to terms with when I found out that all the lovely pet rabbits that I had played with in the gardens of my French relatives were killed for food. I went out one day with my uncle to see his rabbits, and he calmly killed two of them in front of me for supper.

I was quite upset and did not enjoy my meal that evening, and it was something that I would always remember when talking about wildlife management and the need for food with school parties who came to my Wildlife Centre in Eskdalemuir. The sentimental views that children can hold are very significant when coming to terms with this subject. So the feeling of one twelve-year-old boy on holiday in France that day became of immense value to him many years later when he was talking to twelve-year-olds in Scotland.

Such is the value of travel, customs, attitudes and education. It turned out that my mother's holiday in her homeland, to see the family and friends she had left behind when she married and emigrated to Scotland in 1918, was fortunately timed, as she shortly afterwards became seriously ill, and soon after our return she died as a result of kidney failure, leaving me, the youngest member of the family, quite devastated. It was only with the understanding of everyone in our close-knit community, and in particular the love and devotion of my sister Jean and brother Jack, that I gradually came to terms with the loss, although I felt very shy and unable to communicate with strangers for several years, until I started my working life.

As a boy I had an insatiable desire to learn and enquire, and find opportunities to immerse myself in the professional management of the countryside. Our paramount reason for shooting was management and protection, especially when it involved species such as rats, carrion crows, magpies, foxes and so on. There were annual culls for general conservation reasons, but in some cases a purge was mainly intended to swell the numbers of game-birds. This had to be achieved by natural regeneration of the wild stock, as no artificial game-bird rearing was permitted. Conservation, predation control and game shooting had to go hand in hand.

A good example of this came in 1944, when my father was out with a shooting party. Two strange birds were observed, one like a small buzzard with a distinct white bar across the base of its tail, while the other had a lovely light-blue plumage. Both birds repeatedly dived at the guns and my father had to prevent one man from shooting them as 'specimens', because they had never been seen there before. When he returned to the house he consulted his bird book and realised that they had witnessed something special that day. The hen harrier was back and nesting in Scotland. It would be a few more years before the 'experts' would find them, so these beautiful birds had an undisturbed period to get themselves established. Without the control of the egg-eating crows and foxes on that moor, the harriers' eggs or young would have just been another breakfast for a predator.

One of my tasks on Saturdays was to go out with the shooting parties, help to carry the game for them, and learn how to supervise them for their own safety, ensuring that shooting etiquette was observed. It took me many years on the hills and moors with these parties to develop the confidence and respect necessary for effective supervision. Shooting etiquette has been developed so that the stalker or gamekeeper can maintain the correct degree of safe control over the shooting party, and sadly this is a matter often neglected in these days of commercial sporting exploitation. My father always said that supervision and deer-stalking had one thing in common: if you can appear to make it look simple, then you are doing it right. Always be fair, firm and fearless. Safety, and respect for the quarry, always take priority over the guests' opinions and preferences.

At this time we held the Forestry Commission in highest esteem, because we saw it as representing State land ownership for the people, and offering extensive possibilities for wildlife management work. Sadly, we became disappointed at the foresters' lack of vision in this respect, as their original brief for the Uplands was only to grow softwood trees, and everything else was unimportant. Fortunately, and at long last, this attitude has now changed.

My father was a stalker of the highest calibre, and all the years I spent with him illustrated to me his enormous understanding of deer. It was his ability to predict what they would do in any given situation that meant that no deer was safe from him if he really wanted to shoot it. He could spy them far off on a hillside, and pick out the particular animal he wanted to cull. After this decision, all the other deer in the herd were safe, as he would focus on the particular beast he wanted, and not change his mind if things went wrong.

He would then pick out the hidden points of land that were out of sight, and use them to get level with or slightly above the herd. When you were with him and left the last vantage point, you seldom saw the deer again until you were within shooting range, as the final approach was out of view of the deer and with the wind in your favour. If pure stealth was not possible, he would make some slight movement that, while it did not actually frighten them, would make them uneasy so that they would move slowly upwind. He would then hurry around the hill in time to ambush them at a chosen spot.

Deer do not like metallic noises. I would often track a stag across rough country with my father, and as we entered an area of high cover and ferns, he would stop and indicate that he could smell the deer close at hand. He would then deliberately lift the bolt of the rifle and snap it down sharply on the breech, making a loud click. He would then pause to ensure the maximum period of suspense, and then smack the bolt down again twice more. The hidden deer, unable to tolerate the suspense, would spring to its feet and run down the hill. My father would take careful aim and give a loud whistle; the stag would stop, and then die instantly.

My father's attitude towards people had developed over some thirty-five years with the royal family. His respect for lords, gentlemen and the numerous senior ranks of the armed forces made him rather vulnerable to exploitation, for he treated all shooting guests as if they were royalty. As in other walks of life, some of these individuals were not worthy of his respect, and as the years went by my generation came to question this attitude and the whole class system with mounting concern. As with so much in life, it is the behaviour of the few that can have a profound effect upon the many. My first memories of this are quite clear.

Quite often members of our shooting parties would get wet on the hill, and my father would bring them into our house for a hot bath. My mother would run around looking after their every need, and she would be left with the wet towels, a flooded floor and a bill for the extra coal that it took to heat the water. Some of the sportsmen appreciated this extra effort, but others took it as just part of the service. Quite often their lunch hamper was brought into the house, and in spite of the wartime rationing it was always substantial, with a great variety of food and drink.

One day there was a large slice of cherry cake left when the gentlemen had finished, and one of them told his girlfriend to give it to me as I had worked so hard carrying the game-bag round the hill. Instead of passing it to me, she took a large bite out of it, and only handed over the remainder on her way out to the car. Even at my tender age I was deeply insulted by her attitude, and was reminded of an appropriate piece of poetry by Robert Burns that I was learning at school:

Is there for honest poverty
That hings his head, an a' that?
The coward slave, we pass him by
We dare be poor for a' that!
For a' that, an a' that.
Our toils obscure, an a' that,
The rank is but the guinea's stamp,
The man's the gowd for a' that.
Then let us pray that come it may
(As come it will for a' that),
That Sense and Worth o'er a' the earth
Shall bear the gree and a' that.
For a' that, an a' that
It's coming yet for a' that,
That man to man the world o'er
Shall brithers be for a' that.

As a result of that girl's greed and behaviour, I always ensured that I would not be influenced by rank or privilege. This became of practical importance when I was responsible for wildlife management over an area that involved more than seventy-five forestry owners. The clients were drawn from many walks of life, and they soon became aware of my honest and equal attitude towards them. With time, my forthright and fair advice was respected by them all. Those of us who have spent years training gun dogs soon learn that pedigree is no guarantee of wisdom or ability. Homo sapiens is no exception to this fact of life.

MY APPRENTICESHIP

Chapter 7

COMRADESHIP AND STEWARDSHIP

I LEFT school in 1951 at the age of fifteen, and started work with the Forestry Commission in the spring of that year, learning the various skills involved in the establishment of new woodlands in the Uplands of Central Scotland. This afforestation was typical of the expansion taking place in response to the Government's policy of increasing home-grown timber production and lessening our dependence on imports. Most of the land purchased by the Forestry Commission was of poor quality, wet and badly drained, having been over-grazed by sheep and cattle for centuries. Good drainage and hardy trees that would flourish on those exposed and impoverished habitats were therefore vital for successful forest establishment and growth. Species from all over the world were tested, and sitka spruce and lodgepole pine were proven to be the most suitable.

Mechanisation, in the form of powerful tractors and special ploughs, was in its infancy, so most ground preparation and planting was done by hand. This required a high degree of physical effort, but the labour-intensive work did provide much-needed employment in rural areas. Trainees like myself could learn the correct use of axes, saws, drainage tools, fencing equipment and grass-cutters only if the older members of the team would pass on their skills. I will always be indebted to them for the professional approach and good humour they showed towards my training during the years I spent with them.

Our work was dictated by weather and season, and so we became accustomed to siding with nature, not struggling against her. For those of us who worked on the land, springtime was always a period of uplifting joy, with the sense of a fresh start to life. The trees would take on their new mantle of countless shades of green as the buds burst into life and opened to provide a new set of lungs which would purify the air for another year.

The winter white of snowdrops would be replaced by the yellow splendour of coltsfoot flowers, followed by primroses. These grew in great profusion on the hillsides, where their delicate yellow heads provided a mantle for each small stream as it babbled and splashed its way down to the green pastures of the farmland far below. Each waterfall formed an attractive step in that direction, as if rejoicing in the new-found freedom from winter's ice and snow.

In spring we transferred our effort from the forest, where we had been digging drains and cutting birch saplings to make fire-beaters that looked like witches' broomsticks. We now had to prepare the local tree nursery for the new seeds gathered from the cones of the previous autumn. One-year-old seedlings were obtained from their beds where they had lain protected from the main rigours of winter and covered with pine branches.

We lifted them gently and re-planted them in rows, like thousands of soldiers on parade. The icy easterly winds ensured that in spite of the sun we were cold and stiff, and our fingers had great difficulty in placing the young trees in their regimented order. To speed up the positioning we used a device called a lining-out board – a long plank that looked like a piano keyboard with every second key missing. The young plants were laid out in the slots with their roots extending from the bottom. When the board was full, a second flat board was folded over the top to hold the trees in place. This was then locked down and the planting board was used to place the roots into a slot that had been made in the soil and levelled with a garden spade.

The little trees would remain in these lines for one or two further years, depending on their rate of growth. During these cold times I can remember looking over the fence at the hardy black-faced sheep grazing on the new grass, and wishing I had a woolly coat like them. My envy was short-lived, because I understood their plight on cold winter's nights as I sat, well fed, in our warm and happy cottage with cosy blankets to cover me at bedtime. I certainly had the better side of life.

Life in the spring was enhanced by the sounds of hundreds of birds preparing to nest in and around the tree nursery as we worked. The growing of the seed we planted and the hatching of the eggs they would lay were all part of nature's bountiful, unselfish generosity in which we all shared.

Soon there would be another familiar sound competing with the melancholy note of the curlew and the shrill, nervous call of the lapwing. A visitor from distant lands had arrived to lay her eggs in someone else's nest: the cuckoo, with its unmistakable call, signalled that our work in the nursery would soon be over, and that we would be heading for the hills as the planting season was with us once again. We set off with our bags full of young trees, now three years old, to place them in their final positions on the newly-prepared hillside. This was a back-breaking task of countless repetitive actions, as the spade cut deep into the earth and the young trees roots were placed under the turf, then stamped firmly into place with a methodical precision that became automatic when the act was performed a thousand times a day. Each square metre of the area was planted with a tree, in straight lines from edge of stream to top of hill, so the planter would cover the entire landscape.

Working in these remote glens, far from roads or people, I was always happy and never alone, being part of the hustling, bustling world of wildlife. As I wanted to understand the birds, animals and plants that surrounded me, I was quite at ease with my surroundings, with natural sounds, scents and movements being a vital part of my life. With the stab of the spade as I made the cut in the ground for the young tree I would often startle a vole. The small and timid creature would sit and look up at me in terror, its heart beating rapidly and its wet eyes fixed upon me. Soon the impulse for survival would overcome paralysed fear, and it would scurry off to the safety of the undergrowth. A screech and a clap of wings from two short-eared owls flying overhead reminded me not only that had I disturbed their prey but that I had entered their nesting territory.

Soon I would find their nest, with its attractive white eggs, as I worked my way through the area. The distant call of a carrion crow as it flew to its secret nest in an old rowan tree in the valley below warned me that I would have to return there at the weekend and deal with this pest, or the eggs of the owl and other birds would be eaten by the scavenging predator.

As I planted the rows of trees, my slow advance took me uphill though a variety of soils and habitats, from the rich, wet stream-sides with their succulent fescue grasses, buttercups and cowslips, onto the thistles, through mixtures of rushes and sedges, with violets and bracken betraying the presence of good brown earth below. Then, near the hilltops, there were heathers, and also useless patches of molinia grass – the product of over-grazing the land, with its wet climate, which caused serious leaching of the soils over generations.

The hills, with their deep peat and heathland habitats, were the territory of the cock red grouse. He would be quite upset at my intrusion, shouting at me with his distinctive call of 'Go-back! Go-back! Go-back! Go-back!' With hindsight, I can see there was some sense in what he said, as the small American trees I planted that day would kill the heather in just a few more years, depriving him of the shoots that were vital to his survival. Ironically, as those sitka trees were in heather and deep peat, which should have been planted with Scots pine, they would not grow into a profitable crop without the further support of expensive fertilisers and herbicides.

By midday, it was only a short walk to the top of the highest hill, and the view was well worth the effort of getting there. With a flask of tea and some bread and cheese, I was king of all I surveyed. Looking to the north I could see Ben Lomond and Ben Arthur, better known to mountaineers as 'The Cobbler', and famous for its rock climbing. Slightly to the east, Ben Venue nestled in all her glory. Far below in the west lay Loch Lomond, whose beauty has inspired so many songs. Finally my eye was caught by the shimmering of the only lake in Scotland, 'The Lake of Monteith', where Mary Queen of Scots was kept prisoner as a girl, surrounded by the bog lands of Flanders Moss that lead the way to Stirling Castle and Bannockburn, where Wallace bled and the English fled and Bruce in triumph led Scotland for a few more years.

Before long it was time to return to more important matters, with five hundred trees still to plant before the end of the day; but one hour of peaceful meditation relaxed the aching back and recharged the body. Fortunate are those who work on the land when the weather is kind. God help the coal-miner in his black burrow and the car-worker on his soul-destroying assembly line. However, each man's lot is a personal affair, and perhaps such townsmen would not choose to change places with me. One man's meat may be another man's poison.

Summer came, and with it the young fronds of bracken that look so attractive as a light-green backdrop to the swathes of hyacinths in their mystic blue reaching for the sky, watered by the warm summer rain. But bracken soon covers the ground in a thick canopy of death, excluding the sunlight and killing all the vegetation below. This unpalatable fern is well named 'the curse of the uplands'. Our main work at this time of the year was

Nest boxes assist in conservation, providing a helping hand to nature for that moment in time.

He built it himself!   Our first kestrel nest at Eskdalemuir in 1971.

Same box – nearly fledged.

Short-tailed vole damage to young trees.

Short-tailed vole, and below – the vole's predator – the short-eared owl.

Wildlife management is a matter of informed assistance to protect the vulnerable.

Nest of short-eared owl, with eggs destroyed by –
The carrion crow, which is a voracious egg-eater.

Wildlife management and scientific study went hand-in-hand in Eskdalemuir. The wildlife manager controls the crows, therefore increased owl numbers, assisting in the control of voles. Adult kestrel is also a predator of the vole.

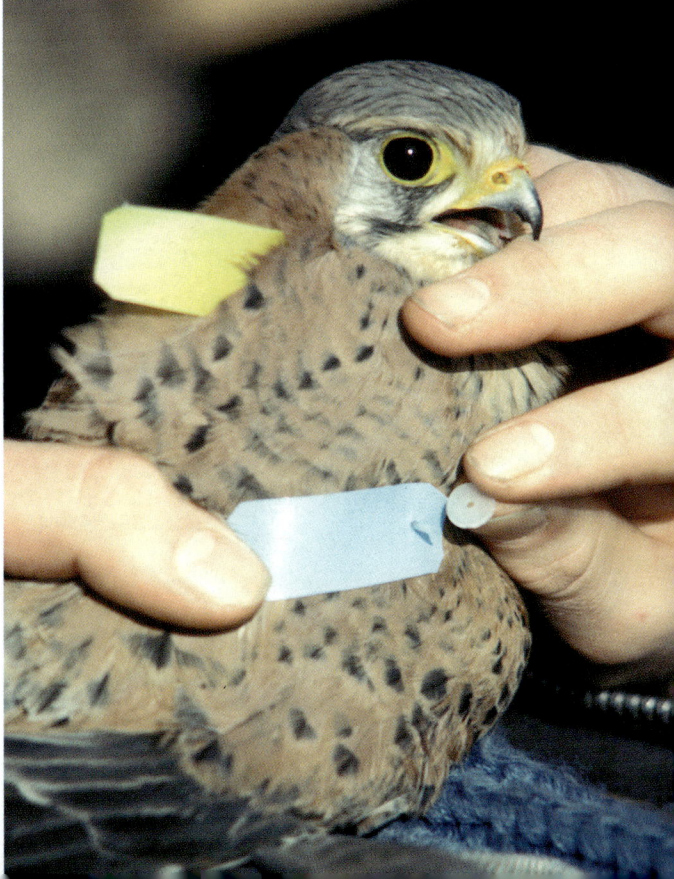

Ponds sustain wetland habitats, providing food for passing visitors and long-stay residents, also improving the landscape. Conservation is a matter of balance in an unnatural world.

Heron on sitka spruce.   Common spotted orchid.

Common frogs – food for the heron – are heavily dependant on suitable pond sites.

Mink control is an essential part of conservation.

Healthy streams are the arteries of the countryside.

Grey wagtail feeding the next generation.
Highland rivers are highways to the sea.

Dippers are indicators of water purity.

Brown trout can provide frustration and meditation.

Seatrout must have access to the upland spawning grounds.
The capercaillie requires effective pest control and habitat management.

Capercaillie and other ground-nesting birds are exposed to attack from several predators. Forest edge is ideal 'caper' habitat. Red deer evolved as woodland dwellers; treeless mountains provide a hostile environment.

Predation by buzzard, fox and pine marten threaten the future survival of our capercaillie and black grouse.

The Highland landscapes favoured by tourists are manicured and maintained by herds of red deer. Red deer forests are upland conservation areas; too few deer can reduce upland to scrub woodland.

Deer-stalkers are upland wildlife managers.

Stress, starvation and death can be caused by public disturbance when the hills are white with snow.

EFG Wildlife Management Team, 1991 (Eskdalemuir & Borders)
Back row left to right: Nigel Yates, Callum Ferguson, Alan MacLean, Peter Kirk, John Wykes.
Front row: Kenny Wright, R.D. Rose, R.R. Rose, Gareth Rae, Bob Smith.

Current Balmoral stalkers.
Back row left to right: Ronnie Rose, David Scimgeour, Bill Mearns, Donald Reid, Duncan Watt, Ben Fernie,
Gary Coutts, Peter Ord (Factor).   Front row: Philip Fernie, Arthur Fernie, George Main, Robbie Elliot.

to locate the young trees beneath it and cut them free with a sickle to prevent them being choked to death.

The main pests that afflict the forest worker at this time are the flies and mosquitoes that continually buzz around your head, and in some humid and warm conditions they can force you to run for cover. The repellents we had merely seemed to add gravy to the meal, as the infamous Scottish midge devoured it with relish.

In autumn, as the green on the hillside turned to gingery brown, the roaring of red deer stags in the cold morning air heralded the start of winter, when our work would revert to draining, fencing and tree-cutting. Later, when the earth was frozen like a rock and covered in a white mantle of snow, we would go to the thickest parts of the forest to trim the branches from the bottom half of the maturing tree crop.

As the youngest member of this team I had a special task that I enjoyed very much. One hour before our midday break I would gather the dry branches from the nearest larch trees, clear an area of snow and pile the branches to form a small fire. Once the embers were red I would collect all the lunch tins and place the cheese sandwiches on a piece of fencing wire and toast them for everyone. Even to this day the smell of toasted cheese reminds me of those happy times.

Travel for me was limited, as transport of the type that teenagers take for granted today was not available. Most people had bicycles or motor cycles, but cars were quite rare and not owned or used much for recreation. The bus was the only way to get to town, although the service then was much better than we have in the rural areas now. Unfortunately the cash to pay fares was not very plentiful.

My main outing was a monthly trip to the cinema in Stirling, and I had a marvellous holiday once a year when I went to stay with my oldest brother in Braemar. Dave at this time was recovering from severe war wounds, having been hit by some seventeen fragments of shrapnel when the 51st Highland Division landed in Sicily. He was working as a contractor for the large sporting estates in upper Deeside, and helping to clear up the mess made of the Caledonian pine forests by the Government timber authority, who had brought over lumberjacks from Newfoundland to cut the trees for the war effort. The result had been to vandalise priceless habitats: the forests of Deeside never recovered, and many of those exploited hillsides still suffer as a sad monument to the war.

All my summer holidays from school and later from work were spent in this area, gradually gaining valuable experience in the fundamental management techniques involved in the long-term maintenance of these important forests. They were managed by the local landowners who had maintained those priceless pine habitats for the benefit of wildlife.

Although the wildlife staff were employed to provide sport in the form of deer-stalking, fishing and game-shooting, their management work benefited all the flora and fauna on the estates. Their casual manner and friendliness often concealed their extreme professionalism, and I consider myself privileged to have drunk at a fountain of knowledge with them.

The bountiful populations of wildlife that still survive on those estates are testimony to their skill. Unfortunately, failure to insist that these forests should be re-planted with Caledonian pine immediately after the war was a costly error that future generations will have to rectify.

I brought this happy and instructive period of my early teenage years to a sudden end when, at the age of seventeen and a half, I volunteered to be a soldier and enlisted in the Gordon Highlanders for 22 years. I was with one of the first units to fly into Cyprus, that troubled island which is still divided to this day, and at the outset I enjoyed the army, which taught me independence and gave me confidence. But after a while as a soldier, the call of the wild became too strong to resist. Happily, the army permitted volunteers like me to change our minds after three years, and so, after three and a half years' service, I was pleased to return to my vocation in wildlife management in the Queen Elizabeth Forest Park, with my own beat to look after and a considerable degree of independence.

During my time away my father had relocated to Duchrie beat in the centre of the Forest Park, creating the opportunity for me to take over his original area. I was delighted to be given the opportunity of managing the wildlife that lived on the forests and hills around the area of my childhood. My local knowledge of the neighbouring ownerships and habitats would also help me greatly in my appointment.

As my older brother David was in charge of the northerly part of this region, the Rose family was in a position to play a major part in the forest protection and wildlife management of the Queen Elizabeth Forest Park. The 'rose among the thorns' had been planted, but had a long hard road to travel.

Chapter 8

CONSERVATION THROUGH OBSERVATION

THE most southerly population of Scottish capercaillie was to be found at the centre of my area of ancient woodland near Duchray Castle. There was an old road that followed the water supply from Loch Katrine to Glasgow, and each year an aggressive cock caper established his territory on this track with such authority that he stopped all traffic.

During the 20 years that I looked after this fascinating bird, strict pest management was vital. I found that as the commercial forest grew to a suitable height, the capercaillie colonised it and bred in areas with a mix of larch and lodgepole pine. My main problem was to guard their eggs from predation within this commercial crop. The caper, at this time, were to be found within an area extending from Loch Ard in the east to Loch Lomond in the west.

I had a large number of black grouse on my beat, and one of the main leks (or mating areas) was on a patch of grass and rushes in a field in front of an old cottage called High Corrie. Before the nesting season each year some thirty birds would frequent this area. It was a wonderful experience on a frosty morning, just as the early sun melted the white frost from the grass, to hear the hissing and gurgling of the cock birds as they paraded in their full splendour of blue-black plumage and blazing red eyebrows. With their large, rounded tail feathers fanned out like the trains of displaying peacocks, the black outer edges of their lyre-shaped tails highlighted by the brilliant white plumage at the centre, they flashed defiance at all intruders by strutting round each other and taking sudden flutter-jumps, leaping and tumbling as they guarded invisible territorial boundaries. They all hoped that on the arrival of a dappled brown greyhen she would favour them with her affections.

In nature's view, a blackcock's position within the lek would indicate to a female that his genes were the strongest and best for the survival of her next clutch of eggs and brood of young. The cock birds, having spent several weeks of squabbling, eventually sorted out their hierarchy, and would greet a newly-arrived greyhen with a crescendo of hissing and bubbling.

Then, as she walked quite casually around the area, each would try to attract her attention by fanning his tail feathers. If the need to reproduce motivated her, she would signal to one particular mature male, who would make a tight circular movement around her with his wings outstretched to the ground, whereupon she would squat down as a final submission before mating.

For over forty years I have been a privileged observer at such lekking scenes, and have witnessed many variations of behaviour. Some display areas are sited in the centre of the forest roads or among stunted trees, but the normal preference is for patches of short grass that face the early sunlight. Once, however, when the winter was prolonged, five cock birds chose the middle of a frozen pond and fought each other until the ice melted and their 'lek' vanished beneath their feet!

These birds' reaction to other wildlife in the vicinity is one of complete indifference. The blackcocks each guard their territory from one another very aggressively, but totally ignore a hare or pheasant that may happen to walk through the lek area. Their aggression towards each other remains long after the greyhens have left to brood their eggs. In fact I have observed them displaying at various times of the year from September to June if the weather was acceptable.

Another fascinating resident was the hen harrier – a relative newcomer to Britain as far as nesting was concerned. I had several pairs on my beat, which had been originally looked after by my father since he had discovered them there in 1945. The male is a dazzlingly spectacular bird, with distinctive powder-blue and white plumage – quite different from the female, which is a dappled brown, with a white band across the base of the tail. Unlike other birds of prey in the Park, a male could have two or three nesting females, all of which he had to feed during the incubation period, and later he helped with the fledglings. The birds were under such strain that in years when the food supply was insufficient, the nests would fail. One of the male's unusual habits was to disappear from the nest sites at sunset, and it took me some considerable time to trace him to a nearby cliff, where several cock harriers had a communal roost.

Harriers have predictable nesting habits, which are important when you are studying them. I remember one male in particular which had a number of hens each year over a four-year period, and I had the pleasure of making a detailed survey of them. It was a joy for me to leave my cottage in the dark of the early morning and go to the rough, open, heathery knolls within the new plantation where the females were nesting.

I would make my way to a good vantage point to the north of the area. Having settled into the deep heather, I would wait for daylight. At first light the meadow-pipit would be chirping to her mate as he searched for spiders on webs still visible and spangled with droplets of early morning dew. Then there would be the nervous chatter of a blackbird as it bustled among the young conifers in search of caterpillars for its mate sitting snugly on her eggs to keep them from the cold morning air.

In the distance the hissing and bubbling of the black grouse as they began their morning ritual display added to the familiar sounds. The repetitive, mournful call of a curlew on the bog-land drew my attention to a fox that was being dive-bombed by this normally shy bird as she did her best to evict it from her nesting area.

I made a mental note of the route the fox was taking for future reference, because if he was not dealt with in the near future, the young of the hen harrier could form an addition to his diet. At this time these harriers were the only recorded nesting pairs on Forestry Commission land, and we gave them full protection.

As the sun began to rise and the warmth of air made the local skylarks soar upwards, the bog myrtle scented the surrounding air with a poignant fragrance that always dominated this area. I poured a cup of tea from my flask and got ready for the highlight of the morning, taking a moment to thank God for the privilege of being in such a place.

Then as usual, at approximately 6am, the cock hen harrier in all his glory was to be seen gracefully approaching from far off to the east. For a few moments I had to contain my curiosity and impatience to determine if he had made his usual kill, as he was too far off for my unaided eyesight to pick out details, and to use binoculars would have been unwise, as the sun would have reflected off the lenses and I would have been immediately detected. The hunter would have aborted his mission, and one of his hens would have gone hungry as a result of my stupidity.

By far the best policy was to lie still. My tweeds and hat would blend into the heather and, I hoped, appear as a harmless object. It would be presumptuous of me to assume that I would be totally unseen, as that bird could spot a mouse at 200 metres. All I could hope for was that he would not identify me as a threat.

My patience and confidence were rewarded as he soared into the sky in front of me. Now I could clearly see a vole grasped in his yellow talons – another item in the food-chain of life.

I had previously found both his hen birds and their nests, and knew that one was sitting on five eggs some 200 metres to my left, while the other, which had seven, was a similar distance to my right. I had recorded their progress as they laid their eggs, which hatched in rotation as a precaution against food-shortage. If necessary, the older chick could survive by eating the smallest one, thus ensuring the continuance of the species.

The spotless, light-blue eggs were laid in quite a rough nest of old dried grasses sheltered by high heather. As the pigment in their shells was exposed to sun and weather, they quickly turned white, and this unfortunately made them all-too-visible from the sky, giving predators such as carrion crows a better chance of spotting them. A predator does not discriminate between rare birds' eggs and common ones. In the interests of conservation, I therefore had to ensure that no crows frequented the area.

The sudden call of the male bird, as he circled above me, signalled the start of his display. His cry prompted a sudden flurry in the heather to my right, as one female took off in a steep upward flight towards her mate. He continued his circular glide, and just as it appeared the two birds would collide in mid-air, they made their spectacular food-pass. As the male opened his talons and the vole fell towards the earth, the hen, with one swift and graceful movement, turned upside down and flew underneath him to grasp her breakfast from the sky.

She then glided to the ground and, perching on a rock near her nest, ate her well-deserved rations, while the male, with a few more excited calls, dipped his wings before soaring out of sight on his way to catch something for his other hen, who had sat on her nest watching the display.

This taught me yet again how little we know about the ways of nature. The male flew over both nests and indicated that he had food by calling down, but each female knew whose turn it was to feed from his precise position in the air.

Both birds can be quite fearless when their nest is in danger from any intruder, including a human. If you persist in approaching them after the first warning swoop overhead, they can drop their talons and rip your scalp open. Each year I had several groups of visitors who had obtained the necessary permits to visit the area, but taking them in to a nest site was not without risks. I had about ten nesting pairs of harriers on my beat, and it was important to understand the temperament of each hen bird.

Some of them were very timid and would desert their nest if disturbed, so for my observers I always picked the most violent pair, who I knew could handle pressure. I would take the visitors to a point some fifty metres from the nest and demonstrate how dangerous the birds could be by standing quite still after the first swoop, and then, a few minutes later, ignore the warning and walk two or three steps forwards into the forbidden territory.

The secret then was to know how to face two attacking birds as they came at my head like fighter aircraft. If I knew them well enough, I could judge their intentions by the flash of their golden eyes as they levelled off right in front of me for the final challenge. At that moment, just as they dropped their talons like the undercarriage of a plane, I would bend my knees, and this would enable them to snatch the deerstalker hat from my head without injuring me. Normally this was enough to convince the students that all hen-harriers were dangerous and should be left alone.

Unfortunately I always got a few 'experts' each year who would approach the nests without permission. They did not know when to bend their knees, and I was always quietly satisfied when they received two or three deep furrows in their scalps. This would usually ensure that the other, more nervous pairs of raptors would be left in peace – an excellent thing, because it is vital that the eggs are not chilled at nesting time due to disturbance.

Almost all my conservation work was viewed by the Forestry Commission as something I could get involved in so long as it did not clash with the job for which I was being paid, which was shooting deer, rabbits, hares and so on. The foresters' remit from the Government – simply to grow softwood trees – gave them a perfect excuse to ignore wildlife management.

This did not stop my brother and me and a few other rangers carrying out the type of conservation work that is much more appreciated in the present political climate. Unfortunately, we were some thirty years ahead of our time, and the yearly payment of £20 from the Royal Society for the Protection of Birds was seen as a small thankyou from fellow conservationists.

The food analysis that we made over an extended period with the various hen harriers throughout our area clearly identified a large variety of prey, from voles to game-birds. Our chief land-use was naturally timber production. Consequently, the fact that large numbers of red and black grouse were annually falling prey to the harriers was not a threat to our business. But it was quite obvious to us at that time that if harriers nested at high densities on red grouse moors or black grouse estates, they most certainly would become a threat to properties which depend on revenue from shooting.

We saw that control of their numbers was vital to the long-term viability of shooting estates – and to the maintenance of the birds' own habitats. If numbers of raptors grew excessive, grouse-shooting would become impossible, the income which sustained the estates would dry up, the heather would deteriorate, the essential food-chain would be broken, and in the long term even the harriers would no longer survive. Negative management is negative conservation, and the consequences are inevitable, regardless of all emotive discussions and well-meant recommendations.

Despite repeated disturbance by ornithologists, hen harrier numbers continued to rise under our protection. By 1964 the raptors' nesting range had reached the side of Loch Lomond, where they were protected by a young Forest Ranger, Peter McMillan, who later became Head Ranger at Queen Elizabeth Forest Park, and is now retired. At this time we had some fourteen pairs of hen harriers nesting annually between us, protected by effective pest control and fed by prey such as meadow-pipits, lapwings and grouse from forest and heath-land.

There are no hen harriers nesting there today – a fact that should be borne firmly in mind by all those who think that birds of prey can be increased merely by introducing legislation to prevent persecution. Raptors cannot live on conservationists' promises or short-term, unnatural, supplementary feeding regimes. Their survival depends on suitable habitat and active husbandry, which in turn requires informed, continuous land stewardship.

Chapter 9

DEER MANAGEMENT

THE very large areas of conifers planted over the Uplands of Scotland between the 1950s and the 1980s created thousands of acres of shelter and good feeding grounds, and this ensured that the deer population would increase dramatically, with red and roe the main threats to the young trees.

In the absence of a wildlife department, and with the managers having no notion that forests should be designed so that deer numbers can be controlled, the population continually increased over forty years, to such an extent that the animals eventually became a major threat to the profitability of the forestry industry – a clear case of self-inflicted injuries. This is now a proven fact.

In 1960, however, I was blissfully unaware of the danger – and in fact I was rather pleased with the situation, as I was obsessed with all things connected with deer. Their behaviour, their food, how to move them, how to shoot them, firearms and so on – all were a major part of my life. I was quite often out on the hill with my dogs and a rifle seven days a week, putting into practice the skills I had been taught by my family of professional deer men.

I am glad to say that they had instilled into me a respect for my quarry, and we kept to our own, self-imposed close-seasons to protect the females, long before limits were laid down by law. We certainly did not follow the general precept of the forest industry that 'the only deer in a forest should be dead deer'. The root cause of the problem was the negative attitude to forest design, deer welfare and effective forest protection.

My three very good deer dogs were in great demand all over the county. I worked them in the forest to move the deer out of thickets onto the open hilltops where the stalkers could get an opportunity to shoot them. My dogs would track and move the deer in complete silence. Dogs that are not properly trained for this purpose will chase the deer around the thick part of a wood in circles, barking their heads off, while the wily old senior hind decides on her next circular run. She will continue to do this until the dogs give up through exhaustion.

One of my most unpleasant but important tasks was tracking wounded deer after those shoots. Sometimes this involved many miles over very rough terrain. Wounded deer will do all they can to put dogs off their scent: they will often walk up the middle of a stream or back-track on rocky ground. It is in such emergencies that the dog-handler becomes an important part of the team.

The years I spent with my dogs at this task taught me how animals react under stress. On a hillside a wounded deer usually took the line of least resistance, and inevitably ended up in water. It would then attempt to put the dogs at a disadvantage by standing in a deep pool, so that the dogs would have to swim if they wanted to approach it. On other occasions, when the streams on the hillside tended to be small, the wounded animal would follow a stream until it found a waterfall, and then stand with its back to it so that the enemy would have to approach from the front.

The deer were unaware that my dogs were not permitted to attack them, but were trained to find and then to stand back and bark, holding them at bay until I could get there and end their suffering with a humane shot from my rifle. Untrained dogs could be badly injured, either by the antlers of a stag or by a chop from the front leg of a hind, which could either kill or break the dog's front legs with one swift blow. To me, this tracking of wounded deer was never sport, but a necessary part of my work, and one which I detested.

I spent more of my time with deer than with people. It was a tragedy to have to kill so many, but I knew that the alternative was far worse as I had witnessed the suffering and slow death of wounded animals. It made me very angry to be placed in this position again and again by someone else's incompetence. I developed strong views about professional acceptability, and the need for higher standards, both in shooting and in all aspects of wildlife management. Suitable firearms and the right types of ammunitions to ensure a humane kill were all part of what I considered essential for wildlife management staff – and indeed for those who shoot any quarry.

Of equal importance, in my view, were respect for nature and a reasonable understanding of the flora and fauna in the Forest Park. But the Rose family's views were not welcomed by the management, who neither knew nor understood the value of such things.

Men who were trained only in conifer production dominated all decisions within the forest. Consequently, the industry lost the respect of many people, who became aware of its limited, blinkered and unwise policies. Of course, the Commission had some excellent forest rangers at this time, but these men were never consulted on matters of policy. Fortunately, this has now largely changed.

Deer drives led to large numbers of animals being wounded. It has always been the theory – put forward by those who know nothing about the subject – that the more riflemen you can deploy in a forest, the more deer you will kill. Experience has demonstrated that the disturbance actually ensures that the cull is smaller. Such drives, so popular in many forest areas, were ineffective at protecting the trees from damage, but they are still practised today by some irresponsible managers.

The suffering they caused, and still cause, is completely unacceptable to me. Perhaps some of the foresters who were so ready to organise these 'fun' events for friends who liked to shoot, should have been with me and my dogs during the terrible moment after they had brought the wounded deer to bay, and I had to ensure its quick departure from the world. If they had witnessed the animal's proud defiance as it stood to face me, despite its painful wounds, and seen that special look in its eyes when I aligned the sights of my rifle and put an end to its pain and fear – if they had been there, they would have been more humble. These are things I will have to live with for the rest of my life.

When I look at Landseer's beautiful painting of this moment, the 'Stag at Bay', I can appreciate his wonderful art but not the tragedy it depicts.

By 1960 the rapid growth of the young conifers was creating ideal habitats for deer. They adjusted their behaviour to take full advantage of the new ground cover, with its abundance of food and shelter. The richer soil types produced the kinds of food they liked best, as the grasses responded to the absence of continual grazing by sheep and cattle.

Unfortunately, within a few years many important conservation and deer-management areas would be lost, as they had all been planted over with conifers. In the naive belief that every square metre must be planted with spruce, no provision was made for lawns, on which the deer could come out to feed, or for coppices of broad-leaves. This tunnel-vision ensured that a golden opportunity of creating a manageable, economically-sound form of forest was lost, and the few enlightened foresters who did question policy were soon passed over for promotion, or found themselves transferred to some remote part of the country.

Fortunately, in the Queen Elizabeth Park, the steep hillsides, the rivers, lochs and cliff edges ensured that all the attempts to create a 100 per cent conifer plantation would fail. During those dark years of un-enlightenment, large areas of birch and oak were felled, killed or under-planted with sitka spruce; but luckily the native trees that grew on remote, inaccessible areas lived on to produce an abundance of seed, and their descendants are there to this day, with landscapes of oak and birch being enjoyed by thousands of tourists who visit the Trossachs and Loch Lomond. The visitors are blissfully unaware that so much time and money were spent in a deliberate attempt to eliminate them.

It was the custom at that time for the foresters to plant most of their areas of rich soil with Norway spruce; but one local forester, David Ross, planted larch on all the areas growing bracken, and so produced the beautiful effect of bright green in spring and russet in autumn that graces Aberfoyle and the David Marshall Lodge to this day. Unfortunately, many other areas which did not have the advantages of such rugged terrain were covered in a uniform blanket of dark green.

In some places nature herself gave a helping hand to create deer lawns of her own. The local deer which were already visiting those areas, drawn by their favourite foods, browsed the young trees down and restricted their growth, maintaining them as nothing more than miniature Christmas trees. When sitka spruce was planted on similar soils, the young trees grew rapidly but were badly damaged by frost, which gradually turned them into 'bonsai'. As a result, some of the prime areas that should have been left unplanted by human design were actually redesigned by nature.

By making use of those glades and the unplanted tops of the surrounding land, my brother Dave and I, who worked our two beats as a single unit, could achieve an annual cull of over 500 hundred deer, mostly red in the early years but with roe increasing until they formed the majority of our cull. As we travelled throughout the district helping other members of staff, we often added a further two hundred deer to our annual total.

Because a large part of our time was spent working with deer, we developed many techniques that enabled us to achieve high annual culls. The key to our success was our ability to predict the herds' behaviour and to set out a calculated plan before we started. The hillsides, perimeter fences, wind-direction, ground-cover, snow and frost were all important considerations.

The next step was to decide if the red deer we were watching were local, or a new herd that had just arrived from the outside through a hole in the perimeter fence. This was essential, because hill deer and woodland deer behave in a totally different manner when disturbed.

If the deer were newcomers, they would run for the hill above the tree-line and turn into the wind, decisions being taken by a leading hind. In this event, detailed knowledge of the perimeter fence was essential, as one of us had to scramble to the nearest ridge commanding the point of entry and be in a position to shoot the leading hind on her arrival. Wind direction played a vital role in this decision. I would run to a pre-established position before the deer reached it, and this could mean a two-mile sprint. We never used dogs for these exercises, as they would have moved the deer too fast and not given them time to behave in a natural manner which we could predict. We could usually tell if the deer we saw were residents, for they tended to lie in particular spots in the forest, and we knew most of the local herds by a stag with a deformed antler or an animal with an unusual mark resulting from injury.

Localised deer were more inclined to run downhill into the trees or the nearest cover. Although they could be influenced by wind direction, they would go inwards rather than outwards, heading for some secluded thicket which they knew well, their intention being to lie up there until the danger had passed.

When we had to deal with this type of woodland deer, our dogs were essential. They were selectively bred for tracking and moving deer, and acquired a natural ability to think and act for themselves, since much of their work took place in dense forests far from their masters. They had to enter the thicket at a particular point downwind of the herd, and on the word of command run in and gently move the deer from their hiding place, just like a flock of sheep. Several miles distant round the hillside, I, my brother and other rangers would be lying in wait, on shooting knolls well known to all of us.

We had no radios, so we kept in touch by signalling at prearranged times from certain points high up on the hillside that could be seen though the binoculars. This was important, as the deer did not always move as we had predicted; but, by the use of hand-signals or a pre-arranged shot, we could understand each other, and often our roles would be reversed, with the beater becoming the ambusher.

The dogs had to be able to follow a wounded deer in preference to all others, even when the line they were on had been criss-crossed by numerous other animals. In all of this the most exhausting task was extracting carcasses from the remotest areas, as most of them had to be pulled or carried out without any consideration of the effect it was having on our long-term welfare.

There was no thought of health and safety in those days. When we were shooting a large number of deer on the open hilltops we could call upon an excellent horseman called John Macaulie, who could lead his Garron ponies though bogs, rock and slippery faces with the greatest of skill, each pulling a sledge with several carcasses on it.

My brother and I travelled all over the countryside from Loch Lomond to Ballachulish, helping other forest rangers with their deer problems. It was a great opportunity to visit many beautiful parts of Scotland and see its landscapes from the tops of the mountains. The sights and sounds would gradually influence my thinking over the years, and call into question the dedication and respect I had at that time for the Forestry Commission.

On the domestic front, this period of my life was without doubt the happiest of all. I had met and married my wife Florence, whose love, support and advice would play a vital role in my future. We were blessed with three lovely children who would add to this family love, friendship and affection that grew as the years passed.

Yet gradually I came to realise that what I was doing was wrong. The system of forestry of which I was a part was no longer a caring, sharing, land-stewardship, as it had once been. Instead, it had become a bureaucratic, politically-dominated regime that was unwilling to change. In my naïve, youthful enthusiasm for the system, I had been converted from a manager of wildlife and conservation into a professional assassin.

My dissatisfaction grew slowly. It is never a simple matter to accept that you are wrong – and it was particularly hard for me, because my work was my life, and my vocation demanded 100 per cent commitment and positive thinking.

The first incident that unsettled me happened in the early 1960s – the 'massacre of Glen Etive'. Since deer rather than people were the victims, it never became as well-known or notorious as the slaughter that had taken place in nearby Glencoe in 1692. Nevertheless, there were some similarities, since both massacres were ordered by government departments that did not understand local conditions, and both were carried out by persons employed and directed by government bureaucrats.

The Commission's aim was to provide a reliable and cheap source of timber for the nation, and already the Roses' views on bio-diversity and sustainability were anathema to the chiefs. The forest at Glen Etive would provide none of the sustainability or wildlife diversity in which we believed.

With its remoteness, poor access and large number of red deer, it was simply not a profitable commercial proposition. A fence had been erected around the new plantation, and considerable efforts had been made to evict the large number of deer in the area. My brother and I were told that we had to travel north, to shoot the residual herd that had refused to leave and was now doing damage to young trees.

On arrival we first had to study the forest maps, as we had not been in the area before. Lying on the north side of the valley that runs from Loch Etive to Glencoe, the woodland's steep, wet, peat-covered hillsides, with numerous rocky outcrops, were typical of the terrain in this part of the Western Highlands.

We could predict the wind, as it would blow either up or down the valley, and on the steep hillsides we could identify the prominent ridges the deer would run to when disturbed. Wanting to leave the glen as quiet as possible till the time was right to carry out our shooting plan, we scanned the ground with our telescopes and identified quite a large number of beasts.

The next day was cold but sunny, with a steady wind, so we decided to carry out our orders and shoot the deer that had been causing the trouble. We placed two riflemen on the lower slopes near the road, to deal with any animals that might descend when we were at the top of the hill (we did not shoot downhill in this type of area, as the bullets might ricochet off the rocks and endanger anyone at the bottom of the glen.)

We made our final plans by picking out, high above us, two prominent rocks to which we would climb, with an estimated time of one hour to get there. The wind being westerly, I would climb the east side and start the deer moving at the appropriate moment.

We made a final check of ammunition, sheath knife, white handkerchief, rope, telescope and a small pack of food for emergencies; we left the remainder of our equipment, including flasks of tea, at the roadside for our return. Rifle slung on my back, staff in hand, off I set up the mountainside at a steady pace, heading for the top with a zigzag route that we used in this type of steep terrain; our leather boots' rows of tackets dug into the hillside with comforting ease.

As I climbed, I occasionally stopped to admire the spectacular scenery that has made this part of Scotland so famous. The cronk of the raven and the cark, cark of the hooded crow added familiar sounds to the wild scene. Underfoot there were clear signs of autumn, and of winter soon to come: the grasses were turning rust-coloured, and tufts of cotton grass had filled the bogs with countless white dots in continual motion, waving in the wind. The scent of bog-myrtle was subdued now after the first frosts, which had luckily killed the demon midge, that blood-sucking little pest that has ruined many a Scottish holiday.

High and far off to the north, above Glencoe, I could see two golden eagles soaring and gliding on invisible thermals. Those royal birds were indeed kings of all they surveyed, with eyesight so powerful that they could spot me, an unwelcome visitor from another place. As I reached the higher ground I found the first signs of deer, their tracks clearly identifiable on the wet grass where they had displaced the droplets of morning dew on their upward journey to the safety of the hilltop. With one glance at the number of slots, I knew that the information we had been given about the number of deer had been completely inaccurate. I could easily identify some 20 deer in this herd, and they would not be alone. Time to unsling the rifle and load the magazine of my .303 with ten rounds.

I had made good progress up the hillside, and could not risk disturbing the deer before our agreed time. My approach would be much slower from now on, as deer in this type of habitat could simply disappear into the landscape amid many shades of colour identical to themselves.

Even an experienced stalker has to approach with caution, using the wind, fresh tracks, droppings, movement and smell to help him gain an advantage and spot the quarry first. Knowledge of deer behaviour is essential, particularly the knowledge that the leading hind will turn the rest of her followers into the wind.

Today, then, they would be on my left. The leader would be lying on a south-easterly slope, in a sheltered spot, while her followers chewed the cud. They would have their backs to the wind so that they could scent danger approaching from behind. These were always the factors uppermost in my mind when I tackled a new area.

After a slow approach around several knolls, I eventually parted some rushes at the edge of a rock, and saw the herd lying in the sun some 200 metres in front of me. It was now time to move them towards my brother without too much haste – a simple matter of a slight movement to give the leading hind a glimpse of trouble, but only enough to cause unease, not enough to alarm or frighten, as that would cause a stampede.

At the first sight of my white handkerchief above the stone the hind's ears pricked up with interest. Two more flashes, and the deer were all on their feet, stiff-legged, alert and nervous. Then suddenly with one gruff bark the leader was off into the west at a trot, with the herd following obediently behind. I knew they had three miles to go, and so would be with my brother in approximately ten minutes' time, with any luck picking up other small groups that they meet along the way.

As I was climbing to my ambush-point, six deliberate shots echoed around the hills from my brother's direction. I knew from experience there would now be an equivalent number of deer lying dead in front of him. As I prepared for their return, knowing they would come back faster than they went, I still had time to observe another part of nature's ways.

As if by magic, at the reports of the rifle the local population of hooded crows arrived overhead, in eager anticipation of a banquet. They had learned from generations of Highland stalking that shots usually mean an abundance of food after a deer has been gralloched, and they arrived right on cue like a flock of vultures.

My attention was soon re-focused on the matter in hand. I could now see quite a large herd on their way back towards me, and I had to do my best to stop them and turn them back. I let them trot to within 30 metres of my position and then with a sharp whistle I brought the leading hind to an abrupt halt. She was dead within a second, and eight others followed in quick succession as I took advantage of their confusion. Nine was the largest number of beasts I would shoot at one time, as I always kept one round in the rifle in reserve, just in case any of the animals got up again and had to be dealt with immediately.

The remainder of the herd turned back to the west and ran into the prepared ambush. I just had time to check the deer I had shot and quickly prepare the carcasses for extraction later on. I bled and gralloched each in turn, to ensure the best quality of venison.

Then off I set at a brisk pace to close the distance between myself and the other rifles, because the remaining deer would break up into small groups as they became leaderless and confused. During that one morning I shot over 35 deer, and when I eventually reached my brother, he had a similar number lying dead in the heather.

Two disillusioned and angry men walked down the mountainside that day. It was not particularly the number of deer we had killed that caused us to question our actions, because it can be necessary at times to make a severe reduction in numbers for the long-term welfare of the herd. What upset us was the fact that we had achieved absolutely nothing in terms of management or tree-protection. The folly of planting a forest in that area, and the complete absence of any design or wildlife management plan, would ensure that the trees would be damaged by deer to such an extent that they would never reach maturity or profitability.

The principles of forest design, and the wildlife management policies that were needed, were still some thirty years in the future. Yet the slaughter of Glen Etive sowed the final seeds of doubt that caused my brother to resign and become a Nature Conservancy warden in the Cairngorms. I stayed on a little longer and attempted to educate my employers, unaware that the time for change was still far off.

Little did we know that, thirty-five years later, two forest rangers would receive a top award in this same district for practising the policies that we were determined to pioneer as a result of our experiences on that day. I am delighted for them and for the changes within the Forestry Commission which enabled this to happen.

The appointment of Bob Mcintosh as Director of the Forestry Commission for Scotland (FCS) on 1st. April 2003 was welcomed by all wildlife managers. I can only hope that his influence will change the role of Forest Ranger from its relatively recent state of deer-shooter to that of wildlife manager. The Forestry Commission Ranger's Handbook clearly states that the duties of a Ranger include pest-management, habitat-management and sustainable deer-management. Mr Mcintosh has already made some significant changes in FCS policy, to revert to this wider approach to forest protection and conservation. Many FCS Rangers are lifelong friends of mine, and they would welcome a full return to a more enlightened wildlife management policy.

Chapter 10

A TIME FOR CHANGE

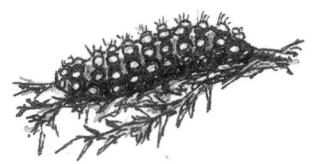

OBSERVATION, information and the keeping of records became increasingly important in my daily routine. Rifle, gun and dog were still with me as vital tools of my work, but habitats, food-chains, behaviour-patterns and the deer's response to my control-methods assumed equal importance. The idea of methodical wildlife management had been born in my mind, and 'pest control', with all its parochial and cynical implications, was gone for ever so far as I was concerned.

Unfortunately, my ideas were not shared by many colleagues at that time. I can remember the stunned silence when I went to the forest office to ask for a map on which to plot deer movements. 'You're paid to kill them, not to look at them,' was the general attitude. I was still shooting quite large numbers of deer, so they decided to humour me. What harm could a map and a few marker-pins make? The dawn of enlightenment had come for me, but unfortunately it took our industry thirty more years to see the light properly.

Evidently, the forest managers thought that I would get over my 'Glen Etive depression' and plough ahead with their shoot-on-sight policy. How wrong they were! There was now a new decoration on the walls of my shooting hut, which had had its walls covered in red and roe deer antlers, rows of fox-brushes and carrion crows' heads. I replaced all these with a forest map with pins inserted to indicate deer shot and sighted.

Nest-sites of hen harrier, buzzard, peregrine and golden eagle were all guarded from egg-collectors and photographers. Plants such as lady's fern, hart's tongue and several rare alpines were all important to me and my work. I now spent hundreds of hours on the hillside and in the forest, just sitting and watching, trying to understand the wildlife. Those observations had a very humbling effect on my attitude, because by this time I had gained a reputation as an effective deer-stalker who enjoyed the challenges that came with each new beat, and I was invited to shoot on numerous new areas, with opportunities to test my abilities to the full. With my skills as a hunter had come confidence and a professional reputation, but proper deer-management was now my main concern.

As I sat watching those deer in their woodland world, I realised that I really knew very little about them. Here came a roe doe, with her delicate nostrils twitching as she scented each piece of grass and plant in front of her. With every sniff of the pollen-laden air she could identify precisely the food plant she wanted to eat that morning, and she would gently pull off the piece she required before moving on to the next part of her territory.

The buck, her constant companion at this time, would walk over to a convenient bunch of willow bushes, and, having selected a suitable branch, would signal his presence to all other males by giving his weight, size and fighting ability in a coded scent message that I could not understand. As an added precaution, he would scrape the ground at the bottom of the bush and urinate on the exposed soil, to emphasise the message that he dominated this territory. Had that buck appeared there in previous years, he would have been dead long before I had taken time to analyse his behaviour.

Each new season rewarded me with job satisfaction. To gain more practical experience of fish, river and loch management I became water bailiff to the Civil Service Fishing Club and the local angling association, who between them had most of the rights in the area. This introduced me to a new species, the freshwater fisherman, that special breed who, during the season in all kinds of weather, pit their wits and skill against trout and salmon. In most cases the angler has little success, but occasionally there comes a time when the conditions dictated by nature allow him to succeed. Those moments give such personal pleasure that their psychological value is priceless to each individual. Fishing is a wonderful sport, whose participants may be rich or poor, in ill health or fighting fit: it provides them all with opportunities for enjoyment and success.

It was particularly interesting for me to work with them, as I had been a fisherman since my childhood, although my main motive was always to get food for the table. I would only go fishing when the conditions offered me the best chances of success, so to me these anglers were true sportsmen. I could assist them with local knowledge of the waters, and enforce the club rules that were intended to give all members an equal chance. I had to inspect the permits which provided the revenue to pay for the long-term management of the waters and the welfare of the fish populations.

But it was the management of deer that still dominated my life. With several years of information recorded on my forest maps, I began to detect important similarities and seasonal movements, and realised that I could use my knowledge as an aid towards effective management. I also used large-scale maps of the district to monitor the movements of the birds of prey nesting throughout the forest park. As the numbers of hen harriers increased, I recorded their movements and ringed their young. This provided accurate information and identification, and reports of their movements from neighbouring forest rangers and game-keepers enabled me to keep track of them over a very large area.

Buzzards, kestrels and sparrowhawks were all recorded at a local level, but it was my observations of peregrine falcons that first suggested all was not well with these birds. Each hen would lay its eggs, but often they would be broken or prove infertile. When I sent some of the infertile eggs to a laboratory for analysis, residues from pesticides and sheep dips were found.

While I was involved in this work, another interested observer discovered that the birds' egg-shells had become too thin; and it was the detailed work of Dr. Derek Ratcliffe that alerted us all to the dangers of DDT and Dieldrin. This certainly changed my attitude towards the apparent success of modern farming, with its excessive use of weed-killers, fertilisers and sheep dip.

The numbers of people who visited the forest each weekend gradually escalated to such a level that facilities had to be developed to cater for them. Nature trails were a new concept, and they soon proved to be popular. They also had the beneficial effect of channelling visitors into areas where they would do less harm to vulnerable species. The concept of recreational forest design and use was born.

This type of development was still in its early days, and I was lucky to be involved in it. My work taught me how to cater for and communicate with the general public, and to my surprise I found it enjoyable and rewarding. I took on the task of giving nature talks to the large number of schoolchildren visiting Dounan's school camp at Aberfoyle. I taught them what to look for during their walks into the surrounding forests, and explained some of the reasons why the animals and birds were there.

Working with the local Boys' Brigade and scouts, I found it was possible to teach them how to read and identify the signs and sounds that I took for granted. I had mistakenly believed that everyone else understood interrelationships within the countryside. To me it was an open book that could be read if one was taught the language, and understood that everything was intimately bound up with the tapestry of soil types.

It gave me great satisfaction to go out into the hills with these young visitors and witness their delight as they began to understand and enjoy reading nature's book for themselves. The die was cast for me to work with the young, and so in some small way to repay the debt I owed from my own fortunate childhood in the uplands. My own children were growing up at Gartnaul Cottage, near Duchary Castle, and I experienced that special happy sense of fatherhood that can only be appreciated by those who are fortunate enough to be blessed with a family.

Our small-holding had hens, ducks, goats, sheep and cattle. We grew our own vegetables and cut our own hay, so our children were involved with natural things as soon as they could walk. My take-home pay was less than £10 a week, but in relative terms we were millionaires. I taught my son how to fish in the small stream that ran down past the back of our house, where we caught trout for supper. One of my most memorable experiences was when I took him out onto the hills and into a large herd of red deer during the rutting season. We lay together surrounded by stags roaring in all directions, with one in particular some twenty metres in front of us bellowing his defiance at the world. The look of wonder and joy on his young face told me he would follow in my footsteps, and I hoped we would have many such moments together in the future.

With each passing year I found it more difficult to justify the actions of my employers. Despite numerous indications that they were intending to change their attitude and widen their view, they were actually still hell-bent on planting sitka spruce and simply maintaining the status quo.

The goats of Ptarmigan Ridge on Ben Lomond were a good example of the prevailing attitude. There had been wild goats living happily on the north-east side of Loch Lomond since the days of Rob Roy, feeding on the birch and oak of the loch-side in winter and on the upper slopes of Ben Lomond during the summer. Then the Commission decided to plant a conifer forest on the lower slopes, which entailed the cutting-down of much of the oak and birch to make way for the new softwoods. As commercial forests and feral goats cannot co-exist, large numbers had to be shot in an attempt to establish the trees.

Peter Macmillan was the forest ranger charged with the unenviable task of their removal, and I was invited to help him. I will always remember the heart-rending bleating as we shot them out of their home – an area that should have never been planted in the first place – and I vowed I would never shoot a goat again.

The trees will never be of much commercial value, because the access is unsuitable for timber extraction, and the increasing numbers of visitors that will undoubtedly be attracted in future will demand the reinstatement of native, broad-leaved trees. The Commission's attempt to turn the area into a sitka plantation will prove to have been yet another expensive mistake, caused by misguided bureaucracy and unenlightened policies. In spite of our massacre, I am certain the goats will survive, and perhaps become of increasing value as a tourist attraction.

It was this episode with the goats that finally convinced me it was time to go. Happily, one Sunday as I left Aberfoyle church I was met by John Cumberland, Chief Executive of the Economic Forestry Group in Scotland. The encounter eventually led to me being offered and accepting the post of Wildlife Development Officer for his company in the south of Scotland. The Eskdalemuir Experience was about to begin.

ENLIGHTENMENT

Chapter 11

ESKDALEMUIR

IN 1965 the Economic Forestry Group acquired large areas on the upper slopes of the Esk valley in Dumfriess-shire, with the intention of establishing a huge commercial forest on the bare, rolling hills of what had been upland sheep farms. In due course the Eskdalemuir estate extended to some 50,000 acres, divided into a number of private woodland properties, managed by EFG on behalf of the individual owners.

In 1969 I was approached by EFG to take on the role of the senior wildlife manager for Southern Scotland (including the Eskdalemuir estate) and Northern England. This appointment was a new concept in the British forest industry, as EFG was the first major group to introduce the idea of having a full-time, professional manager to look after and control wildlife within forest boundaries.

Accepting the challenge, I moved from Aberfoyle to a farm house in the centre of Eskdalemuir – and I look back on my first year there with a mixture of joy and sadness. The joy came from being part of a new frontier, with all the hustle and bustle of change. Large caterpillar tractors were already ploughing the hillsides, earth-moving machines were making miles of new hill roads, dozens of men were planting trees by the thousand, and a new landscape was developing before my eyes. The sights and the sounds brought back memories of my boyhood, when the foundations of the Queen Elizabeth Forest Park had been laid.

Sadness came from my first visit to the upper valleys, with their empty houses standing silent, desolate and sad. Having just moved south from a similar small farm, I felt for the people who had struggled to live on those cold hills. The fact was that the land had been grazed by sheep for so long that it had become dangerously infested with ticks. There was a problem with tick-borne diseases, and in attempts to combat it, more and more toxic chemicals had been used. At the same time, there was a slump in the market for lamb and mutton. Farming, in short, had become almost impossible.

I sat there imagining the sounds of life that were gone forever, like a snowflake on a river: the cries of happy children at play, or their laughter as they walked to school; the bleating of lambs each springtime as they called to their mothers, and the reassuring, deep replies, which let them know they were not lost in this strange new world after all. I thought of the empty, well-chewed box or barrel at the door where generations of intelligent, hard-working collies had slept the night. Names like Moss, Nell, and Jip, and commands like 'Waybye!', 'Come in a hint!' and 'Lay go!' had crackled in the morning air as the shepherds worked their dogs.

We found an old hen-house by the stream-side, where ducks and chickens had been a vital source of food. In the past the patch of rhubarb, now rank through lack of use, had gone to the making of countless jars of jam, and the rest of the garden was covered in nettles and docks growing profusely in the dark, rich soil, where for generations potatoes, cabbages and turnips had provided the household with pure nourishment from mother earth.

When I went into a barn and looked up at the beams of the roof, I saw they were covered with tickets from local shows – 'First Prize', 'Highly Commended', all records of champion sheep at the annual fair, exhibited with pride and joy by people now gone. I was prompted to think about my predecessors in the north, who only a few generations before had been evicted from their homes to make way for sheep from the south. At least the families who had gone from the southern Uplands had not been transported to exile in far-off lands. But history had still repeated itself in the name of that master, Progress, who has no conscience or respect for man or beast.

With the State forestry programme costing more and more public money to maintain, the Government had decided that the private sector should be encouraged to put new funds into the industry, and it therefore introduced tax-breaks, to stimulate the City of London into taking up some of the financial burden. All at once, accountants in the south found that rich men who were paying huge amounts in tax could invest in forestry, get the subsidy and be extremely well rewarded.

Such were the developments that led to the creation of the forest at

Eskdalemuir. The new estates varied greatly in size, but small investors were generally members of a syndicate which owned perhaps 500 hectares. At the other end of the spectrum, really well-to-do individuals were able to take on up to 5,000 hectares each. In all the forest encompassed about eighty estates. Later, there was an increase in foreign owners, who take a long-term view of forestry, and today Austrians have become predominant.

One of my roles during the early 1970s was to persuade the new owners to take a responsible attitude to their forest estates, and the ones who listened to my advice benefited greatly from it. But some companies did exactly the opposite, and it was they who eventually led to the tax-breaks being abolished.

My arrival at Eskdalemuir seemed to me a God-given opportunity to deploy my practical experience and family heritage in new frontiers of afforestation, and in an area that was large enough to respond to my management policies. As I began to make plans for tackling this role, I realised that I was, in fact, taking on two challenges.

One would be to persuade the professionals of the EFG that the then-accepted practice of planting the largest possible area with a single species – sitka spruce – would have to be substantially modified, if my ideas on wildlife conservation were to be accepted. I was, and still am, of the opinion that forestry is extremely important, not only because it supplies naturally-renewable material, but also because it creates habitats for wildlife and purifies the air in a way that cannot be equalled by any other form of land use.

Unfortunately, those responsible for allocating grants and implementing policy were seriously out of touch with nature and its requirements. They simply did not understand that a timber crop must be protected. Failure to plan the original planting with care and forethought, and to undertake the necessary wildlife management, would leave the growing crop of trees vulnerable to serious damage in later years, before the forest came to be harvested, and during its re-establishment. It was quite unrealistic of these people to assume that they could fill the Uplands of Wales, England and Scotland with an exotic tree species and expect the forces of nature not to react and make them pay dearly for their tunnel-vision approach.

In those days all planting programmes and designs had to be approved by a private woodlands officer, and the majority of these, like the good civil servants they were, insisted on the private sector making the same mistakes as the State forest system. They demanded that every square metre had a sitka spruce on it, because any space or conservation design would simply not be eligible for grant aid.

It took a civil servant with vision and an independent mind – a rare creature indeed – to deviate from that hidebound approach. Mike Long was such a man, and when he approved forest grants for the unplanted stream-sides and hilltops of Eskdalemuir, as being necessary parts of forest design for the future, he made history. He should be remembered as the man who changed the face of British upland forestry.

My second challenge would be to persuade the people still living in the area that a new forest would not destroy the environment which many of them had known throughout their lives. The farmers' distrust and dislike of forestry was easy to understand. From their point of view, the trees were displacing them and ending their way of life, so that everyone involved in replacing sheep with conifers was viewed as an unwelcome outsider. It was vital for the newcomers to prove that forestry and upland farming could work together.

To achieve my own aims, I would have to establish good relations and trust with local people. I had already taken the first important step of settling my family and myself in the valley as their new neighbours, thus demonstrating my long-term commitment to the place and its community. The locals soon realised that I was genuine in my concerns for their problems, and as a crofter from the north was able to communicate with them at a practical level.

I also had to demonstrate that I was able to reduce the foxes and carrion crows that were killing sheep and lambs in ever-increasing numbers each year, and represented a major threat to their survival. Soon I was culling large numbers of foxes on the sheep farms that still existed within the new forest, but it was important to let the farmers know this fact and convince them that I was providing the protection I had promised on my arrival.

Anyone arriving in a new area needs the help of some local to do a bit of public-relations work. Geordie, the postman, was such a man. During his daily round he carried supplies to isolated cottages throughout the valley; the delivery of groceries, parcels, letters and local news was all part of his service, and he loved his daily routine. I ensured that when he brought my mail there were large numbers of dead foxes to be seen. Within twenty-four hours the entire valley knew that I could and would look after their livestock. I was then free to bury the foxes on the hill; no further publicity would be necessary, because it was already apparent that the new forest was not going to be the enemy in this respect. When my wife and I attended the local farmers' dance that week, the numerous offers of whisky assured me that Geordie had done a good job.

Happily, the families who had stayed within the main valley of the river Esk decided not to sell their land for forestry, hoping that the fortunes of upland farming would change for the better and permit them to continue their chosen way of life; and I was committed to do all I could to help them. So the Cartners, Dalglieshs, Elliots, Walkers, Glendinnings, Moffats and Scotts became my neighbours and good friends.

Within a few months of my arrival they saw that the staff employed by EFG on behalf of the forest owners could provide a professional and effective service, protecting their livestock from foxes and carrion crows. The farmers made payment by gifting their shooting rights to the wildlife management team under my direction, thereby adding an important sheep-land habitat to my total management area. So another important milestone had been reached, as I had brought farming and forestry together into vital unity for the future.

Elsewhere in the forest industry, the unwillingness of managers to see the light created a public sense of distrust. This allowed deer populations to increase to the stage at which they became a major threat to the practicality of establishing broadleaved trees and implementing the environmentally-friendly design features that the new forest regulations now demand.

I was determined that my work in Eskdalemuir should be directed mainly at the long-term future. I aimed to ensure that the new tax and forestry grant system did not merely turn from mutton to cellulose, or exchange a blanket of sheep for a blanket of trees.

My previous experience had taught me that there was little difference between the basic principles of good commercial forestry and wildlife management, and that the principles applied to any well-run and successful estate in the United Kingdom. The formula I had to implement for the new woodland estate owners was built on well-established principles developed over many generations. The formula had to ensure that the short-term tax situation created in London and applied to the uplands would be to the long-term benefit of all. This could only be achieved if I could build my plans on the harmonious development of the three main pillars of land-use in the valley – hill farming, forestry and recreation. Conservation, co-operation and education would all have important parts to play in my plans for the future. I would have to appoint a management team that contained the necessary experience and commitment to establish my philosophy throughout my divisional area, from Edinburgh in the north to Kendal in the south.

Most of the working population keep regular daily and weekly hours in shops, factories and offices, and could be forgiven for thinking that our outdoor, relatively unregulated life is bliss. For those of us who value and consider wildlife management a privilege with responsibilities, our chosen vocation can never be measured on an hourly rate. Nevertheless, some assessment must be made of its long-term financial value to the estate. This is done by evaluating the cost of protecting the timber investment, which is vital for its sustainability. Farming, recreation and public relations must also be evaluated, though they are hard to quantify on the balance sheet. Since wildlife staff walk round an estate every day of the year, they provide an ideal system of reporting to the forest managers: if a drain is blocked, or a fence is damaged so that sheep can get through, or access by the public is causing fire danger, news of it quickly reaches the office, and so is extremely valuable.

Many wild creatures live on a daily survival basis, with their main movements taking place at dusk and dawn, regardless of mankind's normal working week. They are affected by seasons and the weather, and those of us who work with them must follow suit. We simply have to take advantage of the windows of opportunity dictated by nature's conditions of weather, temperature, hours of daylight and other elemental factors. In other words, unsociable hours are normal practice – and those of us who are married require very sympathetic wives and families, who understand our long and erratic hours of work.

I myself have never been busier than in my first years at Eskdalemuir. I was on the go from before dawn until after dusk. My normal day would start at 5 am, when I met a client who was going to stalk, or went out into the forest on my own. I would come back in for a quick breakfast at 9.30, then visit the Acland Centre to meet whatever visitors we had – maybe a group of students, or a delegation from abroad. After guiding them round the centre, and giving them lunch, I would take them out into the forest to show them whatever elements of our management they were particularly interested in. In the evening I would take the stalking client out on another foray, which ended when darkness fell. This was often my routine for seven days a week, and I believe it demonstrated, if nothing else, my all-consuming passion for wildlife. Besides being deeply involved in a practical way, I devoted much time and effort to compiling long-term records that would help us develop our management plans.

I knew that my work in Eskdalemuir would be at the forefront of change – and sure enough, it came to represent a philosophy that was considered unnecessary and unwelcome by the environmental dinosaurs who dominated the forestry industry in the early days. This meant that the quality and loyalty of my staff were vital, my long-term aim being to teach and cultivate my own team from students with the highest potential ability.

Initially I had to find three fellow-professionals with practical experience and similar attitudes and understanding as myself, so that we could lay the foundations of plans for the future. In the event, I have been extremely fortunate during the past twenty-five years to have had in my team some of the most talented and committed staff that anyone could have wished to work with, and they in turn have had the support of their families.

The first new member of the team was Alasdair MacLeod, whose previous experience had been gained as gamekeeper, water bailiff and forest ranger in the central regions of Scotland. His hard work and dedication during those all-important early years endorsed my faith in his abilities. Next to join us was Alan Kerr, who came from the grouse moors of north-east England. His specialised experience of upland game management and development are still appreciated by the sportsmen who shoot in Eskdalemuir.

I then employed my first student, John Cowen from Dumfries. Our initial training appears to have been effective, as John is now head keeper managing the game on a major Dumfries-shire estate. The next professional to join our team came from the New Forest in south England, where his father and uncle had both been head rangers. Bob Smith had experience of deer management in large woodlands in the south, and he was one of the people who provided me with an important source of knowledge complementary to my own. This gave us a sound practical understanding of deer behaviour over a wide variety of habitats and forest conditions, and it was from his information that our first design features and management plans were developed.

My son Ronald was aged 10 when we came to Eskdalemuir, and it was with the help of this team of committed, experienced professionals that he, as the representative of the next generation of the Rose family, continued his education and keenly followed in his father's footsteps. I was determined to ensure that he received an academic education to complement his direct, practical wildlife experience, as it was obvious to me that proper schooling would be essential for his future. (My own lack of academic qualifications would be seen as unacceptable nowadays.) Luckily, the local school was of such excellence that all my family reaped great benefits later in life. A high proportion of the pupils went on to receive university degrees, and Ronald gained his honours degree in Forestry at Aberdeen University.

To ensure that my management policies for deer were built on sound foundations, we had to make certain that the records we compiled were based on fact. We needed precise information to monitor nature's response to the sudden abundance of food produced by the new forest.

As for the planning of the woodlands, we did that on the ground, rather than from maps, because every site was in some way unique. For example, a space entirely covered with fescue grasses might seem ideal for a deer lawn – and so it was for seven months of the year. But if the grass was going to be covered by snow in winter, it would be of no use to the deer for nearly half the year, and a grassy area which had a heather bank next to it was a better bet. Each area was individually tailored by myself and Bob Smith, and then marked up on our maps.

The number of foxes we culled was astonishing – between 300 and 400 a year. We got most of them as cubs, when we went to the vixens' dens with excellent border terriers in early spring, and many were caught in snares. Then one night in 1972, I and my Head Keeper Alan Kerr were called out at 11pm to deal with two foxes that were killing lambs in front of a shepherd's house. We bundled into our van and drove down the road into a field beside the river, only to find the foxes herding the sheep up against some wire. We couldn't shoot, because they were in among the ewes, and we had to stand there and watch for ten minutes while they killed several lambs.

Then I said to Alan, ' Wait a minute – these foxes are carrying on as if we weren't here. They're paying no attention to the lights.' So next day we equipped ourselves with a headlamp from a snow-plough, and that night, driving round with it, we killed seven foxes with unbelievable ease. That was the start of spotlighting – a huge innovation, set off by one flash of insight. Night-shooting with a lamp and high-velocity rifle is now by far the most efficient method of control, and accounts for 80 per cent of foxes culled. Operators must be professional and skilled – not only good shots, but able to distinguish the eyes of sheep and deer from those of foxes, and they must also have a thorough knowledge of their ground.

We controlled crows – another of our prime targets – by night-shooting, when they were on their nests, and later by Larsen traps – wire cages with two or three separate compartments, in one of which we kept a live decoy. These proved exceedingly efficient, and soon we were accounting for 1,500 crows a year. It was the removal of these predators, which are devils for eating eggs in spring, that allowed numerous other species of birds to re-establish themselves.

Yet perhaps the most remarkable phenomenon of all was the explosion in the roe deer population, which in the first eight years rocketed from twelve resident animals to a total of more than 3,000, as the original animals bred and others poured in from surrounding areas, attracted by the fine new living conditions our work was creating. Soon our cull climbed to 1,000 deer a year – a total maintained over the 25 years during which I managed the area.

By analysing the stomach contents of the deer we shot, we established that some 98 per cent of their food was growing on two types of soil – at first on brown soil, around cultivated areas, and from wet clay, known as soil type 7f , which produces the fescue grasses and the flowers that deer prefer. That was the first breakthrough in our research, and it enabled us to predict where the roe would go to feed. We then had to create areas of grass on 7f soil in various designs. We gave them all identification numbers, and closely observed and analysed them over a period of five years. When we found that Area 51, for example, had produced a record of 30 deer seen or culled, and that another area further upstream had only produced two, we set about finding the difference in design.

This enabled us to eliminate the poorer features and keep the richer ones. This was how we arrived at the conclusion that an area of soil type 7f along the stream sides of 35 to 55 metres width – allowing sunlight to maintain healthy vegetation as the tree canopy closes, and preferably facing south, is the perfect design for deer management. Also a wind funnel effect should be avoided by allowing the trees to grow down to the stream-side every 1,000 metres or so, thus creating sheltered "meadows". As the new plants grew, they produced dense cover, and this proved such ideal habitat for voles that every four or five years a plague of them developed. The creatures literally ate themselves out of house and home, devouring all the vegetation, with the beneficial effect (to us) of clearing away the dead grass.

One fact which we learned was that the cost of protecting the trees from deer could not be covered by income from commercial sporting rents. Clients would certainly pay to come and shoot the roe, but the density of deer needed to make stalking profitable would have been far in excess of what the forest would bear. Effective protection could only be provided by trained deer-managers, and research by accountants now shows clearly that if a forest suffers more than 7 – 9 per cent damage to its timber crop, it justifies the cost of a full-time, professional wildlife manager. At the moment Eskdalemuir leads the country with an average of under 3 per cent damage – while some other replanted areas suffer 80 per cent losses. The new Scottish Forestry Grant Scheme demands that all future woodlands include a high percentage of broadleaves, and this will make it vital that owners get professional help with forest protection.

In the early days we made much use of high seats – boxed-in wooden platforms raised on legs ten or fifteen feet long, which not only give the rifleman a commanding view and place him above the deer's line of sight, but also enable him to shoot safely, downwards into the ground, and kill the deer humanely. But with the ever-increasing strictness of the Health and Safety regulations, such structures have become a liability to landowners, because anyone who is injured falling off one can make a claim, even if he or she is trespassing. Consequently, all seats now have to conform to safety standards, and to have warning safety notices fixed on them. The result is that high seats are used less and less, and those that do survive are as low as possible: the old idea of the high tower is no longer with us. However, there is still a vital need for deer-management boxes on the ground, since they ensure that whoever is shooting remains in the right place, and also is more comfortable during the long waits that are an inevitable feature of culling.

Working with roe taught me a great deal about these beautiful but destructive little deer. Unlike red deer, they are not herd animals, but live mainly in family groups, with a mother and her offspring forming a nucleus around which the other members of the group circulate. Whenever a new area of cover and food is created within a plantation, unplaced roe tend to move in and colonise it. If several does compete for the same territory, they can do severe damage to the young trees, especially in winter and early spring, by browsing off their leading shoots, and so either killing the saplings or turning them into multi-stemmed bushes with little or no timber value.

Favourable conditions inevitably lead to a rapid increase in population. The succulent food growing in a young forest stimulates females into producing two or even three kids a year – and the abundance of food and cover ensures that most of the youngsters survive. But conditions in the forest are never static. Within ten years, as the tree canopy closes and shuts out the light, the ground vegetation dwindles almost to nothing. The does fight to maintain access to the ever-decreasing food supply, and they respond to shortage and stress by producing only one kid, or by dissolving their foetuses internally and becoming barren. The milk of those that do give birth is of such poor quality that their offspring will never grow to their full potential; those that reach maturity may be only half their normal size.

The remaining roe are forced to emigrate – a process filled with danger, for all neighbouring forests will already be fully populated by other deer, which do not welcome immigrants to their territories. Other dangers abound. Barbed-wire fences can rip and tear roe, or hang them by a back leg until they die in agony. On roads, speeding cars and lorries kill thousands of deer every year, and thousands more are shot, or shot at, by irresponsible hunters, who often use illegal weapons such as shotguns and cross-bows. Roe on the move do sometimes find temporary quarters in cereal crops, but when farmers cut the corn at harvest time, they will be on the run again. Those of us who really love deer have no option but to ensure that they are managed for their own good, by planned culling which keeps numbers to a level that every block of woodland can support.

Male roe – bucks – are also a menace to forestry, but for different reasons. They do destroy young trees by browsing, but most of the damage they cause is inflicted by their habit of rubbing their antlers against the stems of broad-leaved saplings – first, in the spring, to remove the velvet, or soft covering, from their newly-grown antlers, and later to mark their territories with deposits from the scent glands in their foreheads. Vigorous rubbing strips the bark from the stems, and kills or maims the trees. To prevent serious damage, the number of bucks in a young plantation forest must be kept fairly low. On the other hand, if a dominant buck is killed, the resulting competition between other bucks will greatly increase local damage, as they all seek to establish territorial rights. Unsupervised trophy-hunting is thus doubly undesirable, as it causes suffering to the deer and poses an extra threat to the trees.

Our culling programme confirmed that shooting the wrong deer in the wrong place positively increases damage, because if you kill a doe, you break the natural process of learning that is passed on from mother to young. If the kids remain, they will do immense damage in their immediate locality. The same applies to culling bucks: if you shoot the master buck in a particular patch of woodland, you remove the deer which was evicting other males, and allow younger animals to move in – and they, as they lay claim to the territory, can cause serious losses by beating up young trees with their antlers.

I decided that the high population of roe deer in the woodlands surrounding our valley required detailed study and analysis. Therefore, I extended the mapping procedures that I had developed at Aberfoyle. We took food samples from the stomachs of deer that we killed, and caught as many young kids as possible, so that we could ear-tag them and find out how far they might travel during their lifetime. Soon we realised that we could make our records even more precise through our programme of tagging: in the best feeding areas we sometimes found young deer within one or two metres of the spot where they had been tagged the year before. We also learnt that the average roe family lived its entire life with a 350-metre radius.

Deer apart, there were numerous puzzles that we had to solve at Eskdalemuir. Why did one area seem perfect for song-birds, while another remained relatively light? Presently we realised that if we planted a copse of more than 25 broad-leaved trees or willow-cuttings, it attracted blackbirds, thrushes and others, and that if we included enough stands of broadleaves among the conifers, they provided enough caterpillars for songbirds to rear their young.

One thing led to another. When the songbirds increased, the sparrowhawks increased. When we made ponds, the water-birds built up. By leaving the stream-sides open to the sun, we encouraged dippers. In short, the entire success of our efforts came from working with nature, and not against it.

The result of large-scale new planting, I felt certain, would be population explosions not only of deer, but of other species too. All young plantations can be damaged by sudden build-ups of various types of wildlife, be they beetle, deer, aphid, vole or rabbit. However, my experience suggested that voles and deer would be the most important challenges during this initial stage.

As for the short-tailed vole – I decided that I would require scientific help, so we asked Edinburgh University to supply us with a PhD student who would join our wildlife team for an initial five years and supply us with the scientific facts to help with the management policies I made for the future.

Eskdalemuir proved to be the turning point in upland forest practice, and I was privileged to be one of several people who laid the foundations. John Cumberland, who made me part of the team, Muir Black and Roger Jackson, who gave me the initial support, and the various sympathetic estate owners who shared and believed in my controversial recommendations all deserve the fullest credit.

Soil analysis, deer management, and the monitoring of flora and fauna were for the first time added to the forest establishment plan. What we developed and achieved has today become best forestry practice. I never dreamed that our work would lead to so many awards and accolades, or that visitors from over 80 nations who heard of this quiet backwater on the upper reaches of the Esk would come to see or study the results we had obtained.

With Florence outside Buckingham Palace with my M.B.E.

Chapter 12

ACHIEVING A BALANCE

IN the early stages of my conservation programme two main subjects had to be tackled. The first, as I have said, was to protect the farmers' animals by reducing predators, particularly on the lambing fields and calving areas. The second essential was to record all the information that would enable me to understand and anticipate the countless changes that would take place during the next twenty-five years in this man-made, imported habitat.

I would have to study the response of flora and fauna to my humble attempts at management, and work with nature's support at every opportunity. Because the design of conifer tree planting was wrong, and detrimental to the long-term future of the industry, yet another vital priority was to educate those who could not see the wood for the trees.

The parochial attitude toward forest protection would have to change. My basic philosophy about conservation was, and remains, quite simple – and it does not recognise the often distorted, complicated and politically-motivated arguments put forward by alleged experts.

All of us who are fortunate enough to live on this planet depend for our survival on three major factors that are essential to our future: food, death and reproduction. Good conservation consists of giving these essential factors a helping hand when and if required.

As far as wildlife in Eskdalemuir was concerned, there was no difference. To encourage and sustain the escalating numbers of species of birds and animals, I would have to understand and develop the habitats that provided them with their food and encouraged them to reproduce. When any new species arrived, it would be at its most vulnerable, with long-term establishment taking place if it received protection and found the forest agreeable.

A good example of this was the extermination, in this part of the country, of the corncrake, whose last two nests in the area were destroyed by magpies and mink during my first week at Eskdalemuir. It is a pity that birds and animals cannot read: if they could, we could place a small notice beside each nest to say, 'Please don't eat these eggs. They belong to a vulnerable species!' I wish it were that simple. Most wildlife is at risk during reproduction, and species with low population-densities or restricted food preferences often need protection.

The term 'pest control' is unfortunate, as most animals or birds become pests as a direct result of man's rape of the countryside and the destruction of its natural balances. Those well-meaning but misinformed people who think we should leave the countryside 'to nature' should have been on earth some thousand years ago. If they had, perhaps they would have been near enough to the soil and survival to have gained a more informed point of view. I often think that the word 'pest' is more appropriate to this group of people. For example, it was the destruction of carnivores such as the bear and wolf that made it essential for humans to manage deer.

Anyone who suggests that the re-introduction of large carnivores would be possible, or an effective means of deer control, displays total ignorance of the present situation in the countryside. We can never recreate the habitats and wildlife of the past, for the opportunity no longer exists. We can, however, create semi-natural habitats and, with intelligent protection and management, maintain much of the wildlife that used to occupy the natural habitats of the past.

'Control' is another inaccurate term, as only the ill-informed think they can control nature. We can, however, make an intelligent effort effectively to manage the wildlife within a given area by implementing a plan that increases the survival of one species by reducing the local population of others.

Success can be achieved only by developing a long-term plan based on local conditions and habitats. In Eskdalemuir we did make substantial improvements – for instance, we increased the number of recorded species of birds by over 300 per cent. The killing of lambs by foxes fell almost to zero in most years, and deer damage to the commercial crop was reduced to an acceptable level.

When sheep or cattle were fenced out of an area of farmland before tree-planting, the grasses that had been grazed for decades grew in great profusion. This created food and cover for numerous species of wildlife that flourished and diversifed during the first five years of afforestation – but to maintain the beneficial reactions, we had to design the new forest in a radically novel way, including broad-leaved species among the conifers, and leaving open spaces along the burn-sides.

In all my planning I had to consider that some 75 per cent of every new plantation at ground level would be deprived of sunlight from year eight to year twenty-five, providing a habitat for some wildlife, but detrimentally affecting most sun-loving flora and fauna.

Wildlife management is simply informed interference or help within those pillars of survival that lends nature a helping hand. It is our ability to think beyond the present, with the capacity to understand and record some of the requirements of other wildlife, that permits us to help nature in numerous ways.

We develop habitats that increase the supply of food, and at the same time we provide nest-sites and limit predators. Good conservation ensures that forests provide us with more than timber, sheep farms with more than sheep and grouse moors with more than grouse.

During the early seventies, my own greatest pleasure was to witness the breeding success of many upland birds which had for years made their annual pilgrimage to the valley to nest, only to have their efforts eliminated by predators. One of the ways I had of monitoring the effects of our policies was to record the breeding-success of a number of ground-nesting birds. I had chosen lapwing, curlew, oyster catcher and short-eared owl, as all these were particularly susceptible to predation. It was heart-warming to see that many of them were now able to hatch their eggs and rear sufficient young to enable them to play their part in the survival of their species. Numerous sightings of small bundles of fluffy down, scurrying around the nesting area as they responded to their mothers' calls, added another dimension to the sights and sounds of the dawn chorus.

In the early stages of our forest development we only had a few mature trees, and the upper ends of many valleys had been left quite treeless by the grazing of generations of sheep. We thus had a perfect example of the fundamental consequences of one of the three pillars of conservation being absent. One spring I found two pairs of kestrel falcons and one pair of long-eared owls nesting on the only mature tree, within a few metres of each other. Both species had an abundance of food, but hardly anywhere to breed – and it was this incident that prompted me to erect nest boxes in treeless areas, as temporary accommodation while the forest was growing.

Initially we put boxes on mature trees that did not have branch formations to permit natural nesting, and on old hilltop sheds that had been used as feed-stores in the past. I also saw that the kestrels were roosting in the numerous quarries hollowed out by the road-builders in their search for material. Normally, I would have made ledges for the birds to nest on, but the quarry walls were so unstable that this was not possible, and instead we fixed wooden boxes to the rock faces. On the floor of the boxes we put soft moss and grass, in the hope that we could provide a safer environment for the eggs – only to find that during the first year the kestrels did not use the boxes at all. Next year we covered the floors with stone and gravel from the quarries: the kestrels laid in them immediately, and successfully reared broods. Of the forty boxes we put out, thirty-seven were used. To make sure the eggs were safe, we cleared magpies and crows from the immediate locality.

Water voles also proved a problem. Although these little vegetarians are normally welcome friends, they sometimes have a bad habit of burrowing holes in the clay banks of rivers. In this instance a number had chosen to live in the main dam of a new pond, and were burrowing into it so vigorously that it was in danger of bursting. I therefore wanted to reduce the group with as little disturbance as possible.

Requiring the assistance of a suitable predator, I had recourse to a family of short-eared owls living some 600 metres up from the dam. For the time being they were happily living on the numerous short-tailed voles in that area. I collected some owl pellets, and by submerging them in water that permitted the undigested bones to sink to the bottom, I got an accurate analysis of their diet – a 100 per cent intake of short-tailed voles. How was I to shift the owls to my problem area?

All animals and birds have a particular behavioural pattern that, if understood, can assist the wildlife manager. Short-eared owls find roosting posts irresistible, particularly in the open type of habitat we then had at Eskdalemuir. I therefore placed several fence-posts at the edge of their hunting area, and in due course further observations established that they were using them regularly. I then moved the posts a bit farther down the valley each week, till eventually they were on the dam. Pellet analysis taken a few days later indicated a diet of water voles, and my problem was soon under control.

An article about this work, published in an American ecology magazine, created so much interest that it prompted two bus-loads of Americans to visit Eskdalemuir the following year to see the pond project that was now history. Luckily I was using similar techniques elsewhere, so the visitors were not disappointed. (Incidentally, there is nothing new about the predilection of birds of prey for alighting on posts, as this was what made the pole trap such a successful killer in the bad old days before it was outlawed.)

One of the worst vole plagues ever recorded devastated the sheep pastures in the Eskdalemuir area in 1890. There were reports of one man killing some 15,000 of the rodents in a month. I myself could remember a plague in the Carron Valley, in Stirlingshire, during 1953, when voles caused extensive damage to a large plantation.

Now, in my new role, I was particularly keen to understand the general relationship between predator and prey, to help develop systems of tree protection. Luckily we had no major plague, but we did get quite high populations of voles at various times, and this gave me an opportunity to observe the results at close quarters. The highest density would build up first on the richer soil types – usually the wet, fescue-bearing areas by the stream-sides. The voles would then spread out up the hillsides in all directions towards the poorer upland soils, where food and vegetation were less abundant, and the reduction in numbers and cover permitted predators to hunt them successfully.

I have seen 40 to 50 birds of prey in the air above those areas at the one time, the majority being kestrels and short-eared owls, with a few merlin falcons reinforcing them. The other two opportunists were herons and carrion crows. The herons would normally sit by a forest drain and spear the voles with their long bills as they ran past. The birds would then swallow them whole with the greatest of ease.

I found the behaviour of the carrion crows quite fascinating as, on arrival, they would all try to hunt like the owls, but without success. They would then withdraw to a suitable place to observe the overall situation, and in particular to watch the young owls who were just learning to hunt by themselves. The crows would then identify the beginners and use them as catchers by letting them snatch a vole, and then, before the young bird could enjoy the fruit of its labour, hit it in the back, making it made it drop its prize. I have seen crows obtain twenty or thirty voles by this method.

I have lovely memories of those times, particularly at the end of a long summer's evening, when I watched as many as twenty-five owls sitting around one of our roadside quarries, with an even larger number of kestrels hovering against the red sunset, enjoying their last meal before the end of the day. The largest number of owls I ever saw at one time was thirty-nine, all sitting along the side of a forest road on a wet and foggy morning.

My observations encouraged us to approach the Nature Conservancy in Edinburgh, who arranged for Andrew Village to study the relationship between the birds of prey and voles, to gain his PhD. His findings provided me with many records and details to back up my general understanding. Andrew was supported by Nigel Charles and Ian Newton, who had considerable expertise of those interrelationships, and always provided practical reality to this scientific study.

This was a refreshing change, as my previous experience of scientific investigators had shown that the majority of them were the ultimate masters in tubular vision. They were always trying to fit nature into a set of rules laid down by previous participants, and were so out of touch with the practical realities of survival that their 'study' always came up with more questions than answers. They provided little or nothing of value for the wildlife manager, as they concentrated on one minor part of the forest for so long that, in reality, they knew more and more about less and less.

As I observed the departure of many of the short-eared owls from their breeding locality each autumn, I was curious to find out where they went. I therefore enlisted the help of the local British Trust for Ornithology ringer, who in 1972 was John Young.

With his help we ringed a number of young at their nests, in particular one group of nine at a nest in Dumfedling on 28 May 1972. My first record came back when one of them was found in Osorno, Palencia, Spain on 1 November that year, and this was followed by returns from France, Belgium and Ireland. It was a good example of the value of this type of recording work, and gave me the satisfaction of making a little contribution to the countryside far beyond my management area.

Birds of prey are at the top of the food chain, and are therefore influenced by the success or failure of their main diet species. Each year migrant birds arrive in quite large numbers to join the smaller resident population, and all then spend a short period assessing the potential prey.

If they determine that plenty of food is available, a large number decide to stay within the area. If they recognise a shortage, the majority will move off to another part of the countryside. Those who stay then choose the best nest sites – the ones which were successful in the previous year. Territorial aggression varies with each bird, and the size of its area usually depends on food availability; but at this stage it is limited by convenience of nesting.

Because such a tremendous amount of rubbish is spoken and written about birds of prey, I should like to put my own observations on record. As raptors increase, they are drawn to shooting estates, because the husbandry there supports a wonderful variety of wildlife. But then, unless the gamekeepers maintain a realistic balance, the raptors increase to such an extent that they threaten the very survival of such sporting properties, which in the end become unviable. The irony is that the birds of prey not only kill or drive away other birds, but eventually themselves perish for lack of food.

Another feature of those early years was the first Outward Bound camp, which I set up for scouts in one of the isolated farm cottages. It was the boys who made the kestrel boxes and placed them in the quarries, and the project had a marvellous effect on them. Not only did they learn a good deal about conservation they were also taught how to make boxes, and how to read maps, so that they could find their way about the forest. Each group had their own number on their boxes, and on parents' day in the summer they were allowed to take their parents to see their boxes, with the young kestrels looking out. Even now, thirty years later, men still come out from the city and the town showing keen interest in wildlife, and knowledge of it – all because they spent a week in the cottage at Eskdalemuir as boys.

The trees in a commercial conifer woodland grow at the rate of about one metre per year – which means that the structure of the forest is continually developing, and wildlife management plans have to be aimed at both present and future conditions. Our records of the nest boxes give quite a good idea of how the habitat has changed over the last thirty-three years.

The majority of the kestrel boxes are now occupied by tawny owls. The blue tit boxes are often occupied by bats, and the merlin falcons that used to nest in the heather when I came to Eskdalemuir now nest in conifer trees. The short-eared owls, once so numerous, have largely been replaced by sparrowhawks and tawny owls, but they return to nest in the areas that are cleared when parts of the forest are harvested or replanted. Ospreys can now be seen hunting over the ponds that we created, and badgers occupy 90 per cent of the original fox dens, leaving vixens to cub under wind-blown conifers.

These are all nature's responses to changes in the food-chain and habitat. It is these practical examples that support my view that design is the vital factor which determines the contribution that woodlands can make to the future of our wildlife and countryside in general. In short, wildlife management is an essential part of forestry investment.

Winifred Cartner was the head teacher at the village school in

Eskdalemuir, and was married to a local farmer, Irving Cartner, who had been an elder of the local church for fifty-five years. They were a widely respected and formidable couple. In many ways Winifred articulated the views of the community, with which she was in close touch.

At a village meeting in 1970 she had expressed her dismay at the damage being inflicted on the community and the countryside by the forestry developments. She spoke for many others in the valley who were concerned by the change of land-use and its impact on the environment. Some years later she showed me a poem that she had written in 1970, at the time of the meeting.

Shadow Over Eskdalemuir

When the trees grow tall, who will be here? We shall be gone.
With sickened gaze we have watched the slow earth-moving
monsters ravage the bleeding soil
Gash upon gory gash. Slowly, insidiously – the regimented rows of spindly
spruces darken the landscape in endless march.
Silent, colourless. No birds sing. No lambs bleat. No children call.

When the trees grow tall, who will be here?
Only a passing caravan, threading its careless way through
forest maze. Only a tight-lipped team of felling squad.
The wheel has turned full circle.
The trees grow tall – and wait – for the executioner.

Winifred Cartner. 1970.

In 1980 I attended another village meeting. I knew that Winifred was due to speak and that she would comment on the development of the forest. I must confess that I was worried by this prospect. By then I knew her well and liked and respected her – but I also knew that she would express her opinions openly and honestly.

She stood up and read the second of her poems. Pride and delight flooded through me as I heard her words. By then her view was widespread in the valley. The poem means a great deal to me: I chose it as the title for this part of this book, for it captures the whole concept of the change in my life.

Eskdalemuir Experience – Enlightenment

*No longer do we see them as invading hosts which march
relentlessly ousting the soft-eyed sheep, the gentle lamb.*

*Rather are they, to our enlightened gaze, myriad vibrant spears
of growth reaching skywards.*

*Beneficent cover to a thousand living things, the deer, the
world of wild-life, the returning birds.*

*The sun tinges with gold the sparkling tree tops, the forest stirs,
a master plan has given it life and purpose.*

Winifred Cartner. 1980.

As I heard Winifred read her poem, I knew that I had overcome the second of the challenges that I faced when I arrived at Eskdalemuir.

Chapter 13

BLACK MAGIC

I HAVE called this chapter 'Black Magic' because it describes my work and experiences at Blackhouse Estate. The place became, for me, a magical one, for it was there that I was able to put into practice all the ideas and theories that I had developed during the years that I had worked at Eskdalemuir

The estate, a large upland sheep farm and grouse moor, was purchased by the Economic Forestry Group in 1985. It lies some miles to the north of Eskdalemuir, in the heart of the Border country in southern Scotland, within an area once known as the Ettrick Forest. At one time it included a large area of natural woodland covering hundreds of square miles, in which Robert the Bruce, William Wallace and the local owner, Black Douglas, were able to hide a thousand men and horses during numerous campaigns against the English. For centuries this land was disputed between England and Scotland. It was here that Robert the Bruce began his war with England, and here that Black Douglas and the Border Reivers fought the English over centuries for the 'Disputable Lands'.

As already explained, I had struggled for years against the old techniques of planting unbroken carpets of sitka spruce across the landscape. My arguments were based on my belief that they were bad, not only for the wildlife but also for the long-term value of the property. In contrast, the Blackhouse estate had the potential to allow the creation of a habitat for wildlife that could be of great value for long-term conservation. Here I could design woods that would support the native wildlife rather than restrict it.

My work at Blackhouse was made possible because the Senior Regional Forest Manager, David Woolfenden, and the Area Forest Manager, Millar Harris, were ready to support my approach. The five owners of the property were also encouraging. With backing from both the forestry professionals and the owners, I had a unique chance to put my ideas into practice.

A project such as this is very long-term and, inevitably, it will be the children of those owners who enjoy the results most fully. I hope that my son will be able to carry on the work that I have started. We are all bound together by ownership and management commitment, with one unifying factor: in the words of the Old Testament, 'We brought nothing into this world, and it is certain we can carry nothing out of it', and if, during our brief visit to this planet, we can make a real contribution by actively supporting conservation, I am sure we can reduce the ever-increasing damage that humans do, threatening to destroy the environment that makes our world habitable for future generations. Although this chapter focuses on the habitat and management vital to the survival of black grouse, it also demonstrates that the future of many other species that live in the Uplands will depend on a similarly enlightened approach.

The owners of the Blackhouse estate have all supported me throughout the years of development, and the prestigious awards and accolades that the project has received are due to their continual encouragement. However, David Beevers, the owner of the largest part of the estate, has had to bear the major financial burden involved in the implementation of the project. He, like my son, is a true conservationist.

His instructions to the management team were quite specific. He wanted to develop an estate where he and his family could spend time, living in the cottage (then derelict) surrounded by as many species of wildlife as possible. He wanted to diversify the habitat to bring back the flora and fauna that were once part of Ettrick Forest. This was music to my ears, especially as it offered an opportunity for conservation generally and for black grouse conservation in particular (then as now an endangered species).

The area surrounding Blackhouse was managed by owners who employed wildlife staff, since their main land-use was for red grouse and sheep; so I was thankful that the essential predator-control which we needed could be achieved in harmony with our neighbours. My team was the one with which I had worked in the development of Eskdalemuir, but I wanted to extend the conservation activities we had developed there and raise them to a higher level.

It should be remembered that, at this time, it was still normal forestry practice to ensure that an exotic tree was planted on every square metre. The challenge for us, now, was to establish whether it was feasible to turn the clock back half a millennium or more, working for joint owners on a project in which financial justification had to involve the planting of many thousands of alien conifers to provide the necessary forest edge, shelter and food for the birds.

My preferred approach, in this work, would have to be to enlist the support of nature to restore the natural habitat wherever possible. However, even nature cannot create and maintain a balanced wildlife community in an enclave surrounded by man-made environments. Our professional, full-time wildlife team had to provide the link, and work with the forestry team and farmers, if we were to achieve the habitat needed for long term conservation.

I studied three aspects of the forest design in particular: soil type, trees and open space. Alex Bryden and his staff produced a soil survey map, David Woolfenden and Millar Harris were responsible for the forestry, while I had to identify areas most important for the long-term conservation of the wildlife.

Black grouse were seen as a priority species. If they are to flourish, these fine birds needs require not only forests, but also substantial areas of unplanted heath-lands. They are essentially birds of the forest edge, and because of this, the creation of good forest edge would be a major factor in our design.

From the soil map I could identify two main nesting sites for greyhens, and also the main sites required by the blackcock for their lekking rituals (described in Chapter 8). By consulting the map, I could choose areas that would grow suitable grass and produce the caterpillars and flies essential to the diet of young black grouse during their first few days after entering the world from their eggs. These stretches of grass, which we created by sowing new seed, could also become control areas for culling deer in the future, as the same soils suit both greyhens and deer.

The next requirement was to enhance the grassy glades by planting numerous broadleaves on the perimeter of each, so that complimentary wildlife, especially ground-nesting birds, would be encouraged to nest throughout the area. Our forest design had to ensure that the trees we planted would help to feed the black grouse, and we therefore established substantial areas of Scots pine and larch, particularly on slopes facing east and south, so that the birds, which prefer to use sunny hillsides, would find them agreeable. Birch trees are also favourites of theirs, and we planted these in small groups. Wherever possible, we left large areas of blaeberry undisturbed, as these plants are important to black grouse for both food and shelter.

Since birds of the forest edge also require upland grasses, and heather in particular, at least 30 per cent of the higher areas of the estate had to be established and managed to provide these types of habitat. This was where our conservation policy could integrate itself successfully with the management necessary for red grouse.

We adopted standard policies of heather management, cutting or burning different areas in a seven-year rotation, and we arranged for a controlled number of sheep to pass from the lowland farms through the forest to the hilltops, to help to maintain overall growth-rates in the heather. This ensured that the plants would have fresh shoots to feed the hen grouse in the spring, improving the fertility of her eggs and the subsequent quality of her offspring. It was therefore important that the health of the sheep should be monitored to make certain that they did not carry diseases fatal to the grouse.

During this very enjoyable period we won a major Laurent Perrier award for the management of wild game, and had the benefit of regular visits from Dr. David Baines, Head of Upland Research at the Game Conservancy Trust and responsible for monitoring and researching black grouse throughout the UK. His advice and support were of enormous value.

During the 1990s, under our management, black grouse numbers at Blackhouse increased substantially, David's annual count of blackcock rising from 40 or 50 in the early days to 111 in 1997. At the same time he reported that the black grouse population elsewhere in the region was suffering a rapid decline. In his report on the first ten years of our project he commented:

'That such high black grouse densities have been attained at this site is simply a result of the imaginative planting programme of scattered pine and larch on the steeper slopes. For this reason, black grouse have persisted at this site for much longer than is usually the case within new woodlands.'

It is always gratifying to me when a project leader such as Dr. Baines agrees with my ideas on wildlife management. Conservation in the future will depend on the ability of scientists and practical wildlife managers to work together in harmony.

Another part of our project was to develop the wetland habitat, and in pursuit of this we built a new pond at the centre of the estate. Here our experience at Eskdalemuir was put to good use. We made certain that our pond did not block the access of visiting fish by placing it beside the main stream, and during the early stages of construction we built a mound of spruce branches, to provide cover for otters until the reed beds that we had planted were big enough to give the animals shelter. It was very satisfying to note that a dog otter was happy to use this artificial accommodation for hiding during the upland sorties that he made from the valley below, following the fish as they went from the lower reaches up through the valley during times of high water.

We stabilised the banks of many of the burns, strengthening them at vulnerable places, so that long-term management of the water courses could be maintained in an area which, probably as a result of climate change, was increasingly liable to flash flooding. I was pleased to see salmon fry, as well as numerous other types of fish, in the burn – evidence that our policy of planting conifers well back from the water's edge had ensured that the water was not rendered acid by rain draining direct from the pine needles into the water. (Pollution in the atmosphere is collected by the needles of the conifers and, if they are too close to a stream-side, it is washed into the water. If the trees are planted at a suitable distance from the water's edge, the pollution is absorbed into the soil, so that it does not damage aquatic life.)

We also built waterfalls that gave the salmon better access to the higher reaches of the stream. For this we needed the authorisation of the Tweed Water Authority, who not only gave permission but contributed useful advice and help with the design of falls best suited to the salmon that would use them to reach the spawning areas above the new pond.

Scott Young and his team, who locked large stones together to form an effective barrier against erosion, also played an important part in the development of the stream. While we can never truly imitate nature, we can, with the help of skilled workers, sometimes create a suitable copy, even though it is still a humble attempt to imitate the things that she has taken hundreds and thousands of years to fashion on our behalf. I am sure that some distant quarry-master was totally unaware that the large lumps of rock being transported from his works had been now re-sited in a remote glen to make a thing not only of beauty but of high conservation value.

At the centre of our valley we had a large outcrop of rocky ground that had been left particularly as a nesting site area for ring-ouzels, the mountain blackbirds that come each year all the way from Morocco to breed in this remote glen. I was delighted to see the number of nesting pairs there increase by over 100 per cent. The sounds of the curlew, the black grouse, the red grouse and meadow birds such as skylark and pipit all grew in response to our various innovations.

Once the initial planting had been completed, our main task was to monitor the way the forest was evolving and to control predators so that they would not destroy the ground-nesting birds. Initially the hillsides had been largely bare of cover, and foxes and carrion crow in particular could inflict serious damage if left unchecked.

It was encouraging to see that, in the first fifteen years that our plans were in operation, many rowan trees regenerated on the stream-sides where there was a local seed-source. In some remote areas, where no seed had existed at the start of our project, the native broad-leaved trees that we planted had grown well, increasing seed-sources and providing additional food for the birds.

There was also a huge increase of wild flowers colonising the sides of new roads throughout the area: it would appear that the creation of hill roads provides ideal seed-beds for re-establishing many mountain plants. The removal of the sheep had ensured that these could safely establish themselves and flourish to the benefit of everyone concerned.

Some years after the initiation of our project it was possible, on a spring morning, to walk up the bottom of the valley and enjoy the primroses, foxgloves, orchids, meadowsweet and wild thyme that were all reappearing in masses now that the sheep had gone. The air would be alive with insects of all sizes and types, showing that the appropriate food-chains to help overall conservation were well established.

Voles, moths and butterflies, all in ever-increasing numbers, provided the main menu for merlin, short-eared owl, hen harrier and peregrine, all of which were nesting successfully on the estate; the only unfortunate casualties being one pair of dunlin and two pairs of golden plover killed by the local birds of prey. (We found their remains at the nest sites in the autumn).

The roe deer, as anticipated, colonised the entire estate and were now part of the management plan. The sika deer which came in from neighbouring areas had to be strictly controlled, as they represented a major hazard to the establishment of our broad-leaf stands, because of their catholic appetites and their propensity for bark-stripping. Sika are natural tree-eaters, with an enormous capacity for inflicting damage, and a threat to all woodlands, broad-leaved or conifer, of any age. Another reason for eliminating as many as possible is that they mate with red deer, producing hybrids of inferior physique.

Some years after the original pond had been built, we made two more ponds to enlarge the wetland habitat still further. All three became important building-blocks in our development for long term conservation. They soon had a significant impact on the wetland wildlife, so that mallard, teal and dipper were all sharing in the morning's celebrations. The occasional plop of the fish jumping for a fly was a reminder that our local otter – now a frequent visitor – had a good food supply to share with the herons, who had also soon discovered this improvement to their environment.

One of my happiest experiences was sitting by the waterfalls I had helped to build, watching some of David Beevers' grandchildren playing in the water, chasing minnows and frogs among the pebbles, as I had done many years ago. I can only hope that their early memories of such events will be as happy as mine.

As the forest canopy began to close, the light reaching ground level was increasingly restricted. We had always known that this would happen and that it would have a negative affect on the overall wildlife population. Now we had to decide how to deal with this conflict between the economics of forestry and the conservation of wildlife.

A meeting was organised between my son Ronald, David Beevers, David Baines and myself. We discussed the problems we faced and the possible solutions, and then held a number of planning discussions. For these, we brought in David Woolfenden, who had retired some years before and was now assisting David Beevers with his woodland management. A number of important improvements were identified as necessary:

1. The original forest edge had to be moved back and redesigned to provide more space for the black grouse, and the habitat adjusted to provide more food.

2. The forest cover must be reduced so that some 200 acres of valley sides had less than 20 per cent tree-cover, consisting mainly of larch and Scots pine, to ensure that the ground vegetation would re-establish itself in the sunlight and provide large areas of heather and blaeberry.

We tried a number of ways to dispose of the trees (which were too small to have any commercial value). Our first experiment was to burn them, and this was satisfactory to the extent that it completely got rid of the trunks and branches. However, the cost was prohibitive. Next we tried chipping. This also dealt with the wood, but it left a thick carpet of chips which might blanket the soil and reduce growth for some time. It was also expensive. Finally we settled on cutting the surplus trees, brashing them (taking off the branches) and leaving them on the hillside. We were pleasantly surprised to find how quickly the heather grew through and hid the remnants.

3. The lekking sites should be improved by felling the perimeter trees to give clear access to the birds as they flew in during the early morning. Our observations over many years had clearly established that the blackcock favoured low tree-cover. Consequently, we agreed that the cutting of vegetation and, in some cases, the complete removal of the cut trees, would be a major improvement.

4. Many of the sites originally left as vital greyhen nesting areas were being colonised by bracken, and a large bracken- spraying programme had to be initiated.

5. Oats and quinoa were planted as an additional food source in areas where old plots had been cultivated in years gone by, and on some of the richer soils. We also planned to enhance existing food sources such as blaeberry for the black grouse and deer that lived in those particular areas.

When David Beevers obtained a long lease on farmland adjoining Blackhouse, we were able to extend the area which we could control. In particular, we could increase the spaces available as nesting sites for the greyhens. The removal of some large patches of bracken also extended their feeding area.

A second and equally important development was the purchase of a large forest on the eastern boundary of Blackhouse by Kronospan, the well-known timber processors, owned by Mr. M. Kaindl. He and I have the same attitude towards wildlife management and conservation. I was delighted that he gave our conservation plans, and especially our black grouse project, his full support and promised to take any appropriate steps to improve the habitat on his ground.

This was particularly important, as many of the steep hillsides that had been originally colonised by the black grouse were now covered in thick conifers, and a complete re-design would be necessary in the near future. His support can only add to the benefits of our overall success, as it makes a substantial increase to the size of the area under the conservation plans we had started in the 1980s.

Our original plans for the second stage of the Blackhouse project were hit by a dramatic set-back in the form of the foot-and-mouth epidemic of 2001, which meant that we had to call a halt to everything we had planned. We could not even visit the estate for several months. When at last we could meet again on site, we agreed that it was vital that no more time was lost.

We agreed that the project we had planned to complete in three years would have to be completed in one. This was a major challenge. However, with the help and enthusiastic support of all involved, we managed to meet our new timetable.

Blackhouse can now enter the third stage of its management with the best habitat that we could devise for black grouse. In creating this, we were greatly assisted by the help and advice we received from David Baines. His knowledge of these birds is unrivalled in the UK and probably in the world.

As a result of our improvements, the entire area has benefited. An upland habitat has been established by creating woodlands for wildlife and timber which enhance the landscape and give pleasure to all those who visit them. Nature's response to our work has given me great satisfaction: the wealth of wildlife that can now be seen is proof that we took at least one small step in the right direction.

Sadly, the long-term future of black grouse is by no means secure. Reporting on the results of his monitoring, David Baines said:

'Blackhouse aside, local leks have shown a 76 per cent decline in only nine years. This fact illustrates the local, and probably regional, importance of your estate for this species. On a related note, not only has Blackhouse supported higher densities of black grouse than any other site we monitor throughout Britain, but they also bred very successfully there. Hence it is likely that excess young produce will disperse and supplement dwindling numbers in adjacent areas. To put it simply, our data show the site to be the engine room or a pivotal site for black grouse within the local area.'

Clearly Blackhouse is a site of great importance to the survival of this beautiful and increasingly rare bird. Despite all the work that we have done, it is still threatened by predation. The birds have become extinct in much of Europe, and if they are to survive in the UK they must be strictly protected from all types of predator.

Chapter 14

WETLANDS

AS I travel the country and look at many areas of upland forestry, I can identify hundreds of sites where the owners have been misled into putting in expensive and ineffective drainage schemes that will almost inevitably result in the total loss of their investment. The soil and weather in those areas of natural wetland will, quite simply, ensure that no profitable tree crop can ever be harvested.

The commercial forest companies responsible for giving bad advice find that such areas are particularly profitable to them, because they can encourage unsuspecting owners to re-drain and replant the ground with monotonous regularity – all in the interests of company profits rather than for the benefit of the owners themselves. Nature will ensure that no profitable timber can be produced, because forestry is an unsuitable and unsustainable form of land-use in such conditions.

To add insult to injury, in the majority of instances the owner could have created a profitable asset by turning that wet area into a pond, at a fraction of the cost of the ill-advised tree planting, which should never have received a forestry grant. In the future we must hope that the Forest Authority will not pay grants for this type of negative and unproductive land-use. Conservation grants should be paid to owners who are wise enough to see the good sense and value of developing ponds in suitable places.

I will always be grateful to the owners who heeded my advice and permitted me to create important conservation areas in places for which there was no chance of getting grants. The undoubted success of the ponds is a direct result of their financial support, which enabled a team of positively-minded, experienced professionals to create long-term assets for the estates, to the lasting benefit of the countryside and all those who value wildlife.

It is impossible for me fully to express the happiness and satisfaction that I experience when I visit new wetlands and enjoy the sights and sounds of the wildlife – the call of the duck as they return at sunset to join the chorus of croaking frogs, or the plop of a rising fish as it feasts on the abundant flies and moths that have all become part of the man-made ecosystem.

Then there is an occasional special bonus, when I can savour rare moments that most people never see. At first light in the morning there may be the spectacular sight of an osprey hunting as it hovers over the water to identify its breakfast swimming beneath the surface below. Its rapid wing-beats give it complete control in the air, and I wait for its spectacular dive as it closes its wings and drops on its unsuspecting quarry.

The dawn chorus is momentarily interrupted by the splash of the supreme avian fish-predator as it hits the water. I concentrate on the focusing of my video camera as I endeavour to capture this moment for others to enjoy at some later date. With powerful wings the osprey lifts itself off the water, and a wriggling fish is visible, held as in a vice in the bright-yellow talons that glisten and drip with water as they are highlighted by the early morning sun. I struggle to keep the bird in view, as I know from past experience that it will hover and shake itself in mid-air as it attempts to rid its feathers of excess water before it flies off to its chosen perch to feast on its prey.

At times like this I am reminded that, had it not been for my original endeavours in making this pond, the area would now be occupied by a large number of frosted, stunted, bonsai-type sitka spruce, of no commercial value, and indeed of no value at all, especially when compared with the priceless display of predator and prey that I have just witnessed.

I hope that the woodland owner will share this view when he and his friends see the video film. They can be proud of the fact that they have financed the osprey's display by giving nature a helping hand, and by appreciating the satisfaction, enjoyment and financial benefits that can accrue from expenditure on this type of habitat creation and management.

Another advantage of the osprey pond was that it gave us a good frontage from which people in wheelchairs could fish. Among the beneficiaries were patients from a marvellous organisation called Headcare, which helps people recover from serious head injuries. Some of them were only able to sit and watch the wildlife – itself a healing process – but others went much further and learnt to fish. For me, it was immensely rewarding to see someone attain the coordination needed to handle a rod and bring a fish out of the water.

Ponds, like anything else, must be properly designed and built. Poor-quality design and workmanship are commonplace, especially as the foundations and other important features are underwater and out of sight. It is essential that informed supervision takes place during construction, as costly long-term defects can occur during the early stages. I have often known owners who were persuaded by their agents to take the cheapest option in the short term, eventually discover that they have made expensive mistakes. Unfortunately and inevitably, defects almost always become apparent at a later date, when the advisor and his incompetent or inexperienced contractor have long since disappeared.

I hope it will be of interest to all those who find peace and contentment by the waterside if I summarise some of the procedures that I have developed and the records I have kept over the past 35 years. Most of the upland sites I have had to work with were free from pollution, with the exception of isolated places in which sheep had been dipped. These areas could not be flooded because the toxic residues of the past might contaminate the pond water: chemicals like DDT and Dieldrin are very unwelcome ingredients in any conservation project.

The suitability of a local water-source can be established by observing the wildlife in and under the stones in the stream. If freshwater shrimps are found, they indicate positively that the water is uncontaminated. The acidity of the water will be reflected in the types of vegetation most common in the areas upstream from the proposed pond site.

If these primary indications are good, a meeting with the local river authority should take place to verify the findings and discuss the project, so that any recommendations made by local experts can be added to the design and management plan. Soil-profile and local contours will determine the general shape and construction of the pond, and the final placement and size can be determined when the overall catchment area has been assessed.

If a large area of surface water is involved, it is wise to seek the services of an experienced survey team, and gain permission from the local planning authority. Ponds retained by earth dams should only be constructed across small streams if they are situated on or near the watershed of any upland area. All other ponds should be placed at the side of the main stream, to prevent flooding at times of high rainfall or melting snow. Care must be taken at all times to ensure that migratory fish such as salmon and sea trout are not restricted when they travel upstream to their spawning areas.

All dams must be countersunk into the ground and keyed into the bank at each end, with the overflow positioned to resist erosion in years ahead. This can only be achieved by constructing the overflow with a gradual decline, with the water running over rocks or inlaid stones. The depth of a pond is determined by the height of the overflow, of course: it must therefore be able to accommodate high water levels, and be constructed with materials that will not erode.

The perimeter contour of the pond and the heights of the jetties and islands can be established early on. When the costs and feasibility of the project are being considered, I have certain main priorities, because the major part of the expenditure will be determined by the height and length of the retaining wall. It is important to gauge the area of surface water that will be created, and this can be assessed by the use of a level placed on a stand. Natural contours which will retain water, and hollows and valleys that lend themselves to natural damming, are all valuable features. Areas that need major excavation of soil with a gravel base demand substantial capital outlay, and should be considered only if good local clay is available to surface the hollow and make it watertight.

The main consideration in planning any new pond is the contribution it will make to its immediate surroundings by offering a new ecosystem for species not already present. The conservation value of a pond can be measured by considering the acidity of the water supply. Altitude and exposure also affect long-term conservation possibilities.

All wetland habitats are potentially useful conservation areas, but it should be understood that their value does not multiply in direct proportion to the extent of the water surface. For example, the wildlife conservation value of one three-hectare pond is usually not as high as that achieved by creating three one-hectare ponds.

When developing design features to assist in boating or fishing, all materials used should be water-resistant and blend with local surroundings. All the wood used on fish grids, jetties and so on should be ash, Scots pine or larch, and salt-cured as required. All fittings should be galvanised or coated in plastic to prevent corrosion, and all stonework on the face of the dam and slip-ways should be made from local sources. Any pond that will be used for fishing should be fitted with retaining grids on both inlet and outlet, with mesh sizes which permit small, local fish to enter from the stream while retaining larger, introduced species within bounds. All ponds used for fishing should have a life-belt and retaining cord available and prominently displayed at the dam. If the pond is in a forest, a silt trap is essential and should be dug between the inlet and the pond.

The design must include careful consideration of plants that may be introduced to create habitats. Plants that can provide a short, dense habitat should be established at the edges where fishing is the main consideration, while small bays can be planted with reeds. These will create a high, dense undergrowth that will be used by much of the wildlife as a sanctuary in times of disturbance.

It is also essential to understand that a new, man-made pond will only give full value if it is managed on an annual basis, and receives appropriate pest control. For example, the arrival of mink can quickly wipe out much of a site's conservation value, because within a few weeks the predators bring death and destruction to ducks, fish, voles and other species.

The value of all wetland habitats is determined by the amount of food and sanctuary they can provide for passing visitors and permanent residents. For visitors, a bog should be able to supply uncontaminated food on a seasonal basis. Permanently resident creatures need food within easy reach all the year round, so that they can reproduce without excessive predation or stressful disturbance. This can only be fully achieved by good design, effective pest control, and locally-based management.

It is important that native plants are used whenever possible, so that a long-term seed source can be created. Sometimes, due to exposure, time-scale and soil conditions, this is not feasible, but any exotic introduction should be carefully considered to ensure that it does not destroy the native habitat or its wildlife in the longer term.

Unfortunately, there are numerous examples of this happening all over the world. I shall always remember during one of my study tours in Denmark being taken by an old gamekeeper to a large pond on a beautiful sporting estate. From a distance it looked like a perfect conservation area, but when we got to the edge of the water I was amazed to find that it did not have any vegetation, and gave the impression that it had been sprayed with some deadly weed-killer.

My guide told me that the lake had been a key sporting area, which produced hundreds of fish and ducks annually, and had been a wonderland for wildfowl. Unfortunately, the owner had become unhappy with the reeds and water lilies that were interfering with his fishing, and he had responded by introducing some exotic vegetarian carp, which found a perfect food supply but had no predator. The carp therefore bred out of control and destroyed the entire habitat, leaving the pond devastated, a monument to unenlightened introductions and one man's failure to understand nature's workings.

I often disagree with the purists who seek to recreate what is, in practice, unachievable, while our wildlife disappears; and I have always taken the view that the best way forward is the construction and management of semi-natural habitats. I have enjoyed making a small contribution towards a better countryside for our wildlife. When ospreys or otters frequent the ponds and habitats that I have made and go fishing for food, they do not discriminate between our small, native brown trout or the larger Canadian brook trout that I have used for re-stocking in the short term. The laws of survival do not permit them the human privilege and luxury of choosing. It is the availability of food that has attracted them to the pond, and without food they would die.

Otters are also reliant on the reed beds that I have established with the help of nature and the financial support of the owners, who can fish for brook trout while enjoying the other wildlife that their investment has encouraged and sustained.

My main concern is to provide wildlife with food, safety and retreat for the times when homo sapiens and his dogs come to disturb and terrorise the area during their periodic outings to secluded spots. Many people remain blissfully unaware of the damage that an unsupervised dog can do. As always, education, appreciation and understanding are essential for effective conservation. Therefore, design features that can restrict disturbance to 25 per cent in any wildlife area should be sufficient to ensure that nature and the public can co-exist to the benefit of all concerned. The purist can still go on dreaming about the re-creation of the water habitats that were here a thousand years ago but will never, in reality, come again.

The streams and rivers that criss-cross our landscapes are the arteries of life, as the water they carry is essential for our survival. I have always found it rewarding to climb to the top of a high hill and discover the springs that are responsible for much of the wildlife that lives in remote glens. Fortunately, my life in the hills has enabled me to drink from these fountains of life. It is a marvellous experience to taste the clear, cool water that gushes from the heart of Mother Nature, where she has filtered and purified our polluted rain to produce a drink far more refreshing than any of the bottled versions that we buy in super-stores or, indeed, the medicated substitutes

Grouse moors are managed heather habitats, maintained by careful selective burning.
Young heather and upland plant growth is improved by this controlled management.

Unmanaged heather can kill many upland plant species by smothering.

Ring ouzel – an annual visitor to our grouse moors from Morocco.

Dotterel and blue hare – dwellers of the high tops – are vulnerable to disturbance by humans and their dogs.
The blue hare provides nourishment for many predators.

Golden eagles thrive in red deer forests.
Deer fencing is essential where deer forests and woodlands share the same landscape. Removal of fencing in recent times has created unnecessary damage and excessive killing of deer.

Typical deer damage.

All access routes should have suitable gates or stiles.

Deer husbandry employs local people, and provides pure organic venison for the table.

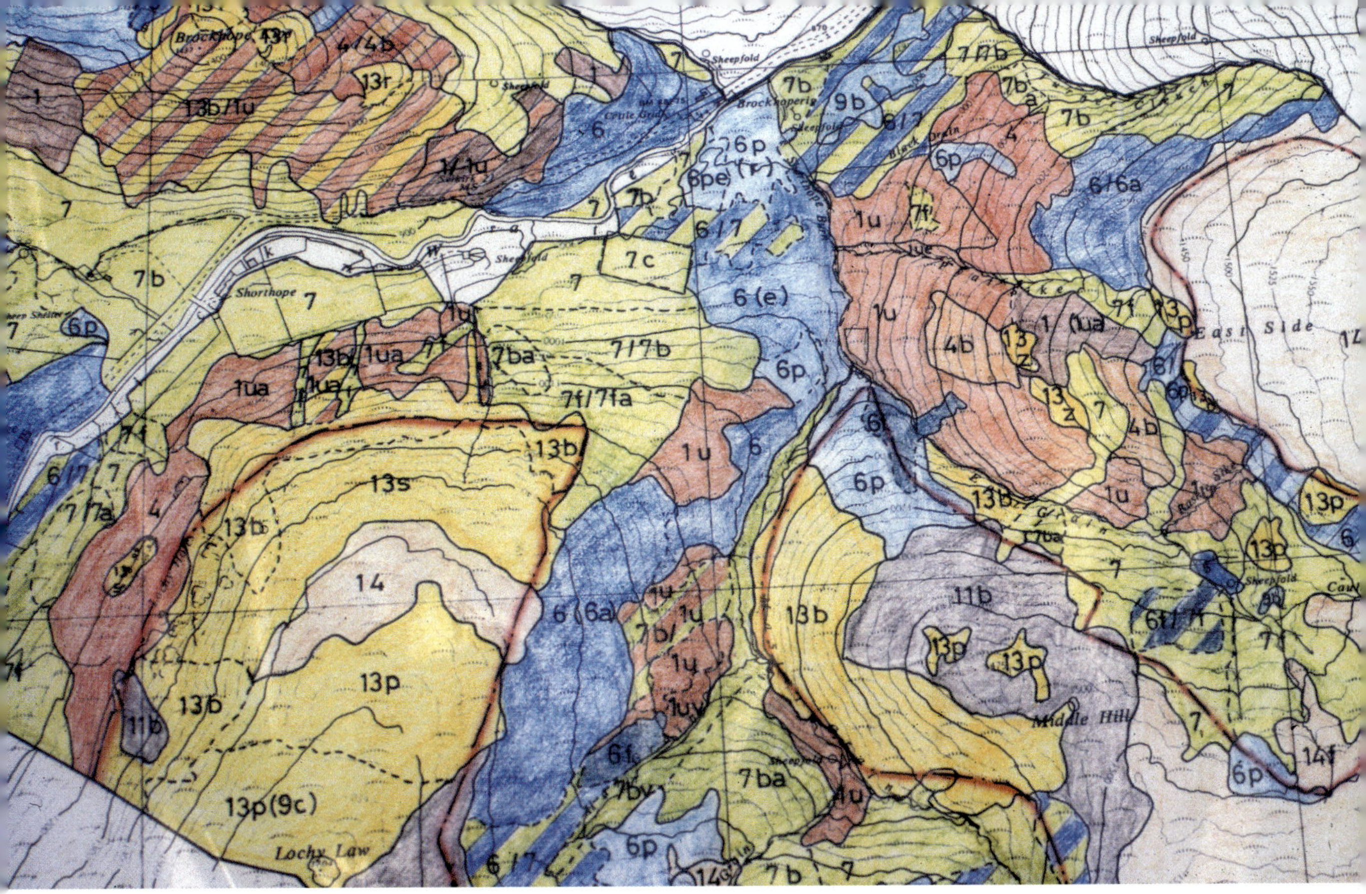

A soil map is a vital part of enlightened forest design.

When farming, forestry and fieldsports walk in harmony, popular tourist landscapes evolve.

Roe deer – the most common woodland deer in Scotland – are selective feeders who live in a world of scent and succulent food vegetation. Excessive numbers can severely damage young trees. Control is essential.

Tree guards are no protection in highly populated areas.

Roe deer twin fawns.

Globe flower, a sign of healthy waterside habitat.

Black cock at the lek.

Roe buck removing velvet.

The grey hen – female black game – requires suitable habitat and protection from predation.
Willows should be provided for roe buck to remove their velvet.

Established woodland is the result of long-term stewardship.

The broad leaves of forest trees nurture the eggs of life.   *Biodiversity has been practiced by sporting estates for centuries.*

Caterpillars from the surrounding trees are the main food supply for small birds.

The mistle thrush is the central part of the food chain.

The sparrowhawk is dependant on food provided by good conservation.

Forest design is an essential part of woodland conservation.
Management policy must stand on a foundation of fact, not fiction.

If we destroy the flowers and insects of our world, we will die. Ignorance, arrogance and greed are the enemies of effective conservation. We borrow our wildlife from our grandchildren.

that come through our taps and are described as drinking water.

We British live in a part of the world where rain is taken for granted, and anyone who drinks from a mountain spring should be truly grateful that he or she is not in a region where lack of water and rain has devastated the countryside and turned green pastures of the past into deserts of the future.

With this in mind, we should view every spring with grateful understanding. So let us take a closer look at this mountain stream as it tumbles its way eventually to the sea – for during its journey it will pass through farm, forest, village and town, all dependent on water for their survival. The summit of the hill above our spring is covered in a thick, close mat of vegetation. Cloudberry, cranberry, mosses and lichens all cling together to cover the rocky outcrop, rooted in small pockets of shallow soil. Only the hardiest of plants can survive the rigours of this high, semi-alpine zone.

Where the spring first sees the light of day on a contour just below the summit, at a point where soil and shelter permit more dense vegetation, it is surrounded by a number of heathers. First, on the rockiest outcrop, there is bell-heather, with its deep purple flowers, which are always the first to bloom in the late springtime at this high altitude. Then, on the wetter part we can see the cross-leaved heather with its delicate, light-pink flowers of single structure that emerge from a bed of mosses and wild cotton. The rest of the area is dominated by the most common heather to be found in Britain – ling, the one that gives the impression that the uplands are purple, as its flowers thrive and bloom in the summer.

The common denominator that determines the welfare of the plants up here is the presence of acid soil from peat and bog. So it is an interesting contrast to look at the plants that surround the spring as it wells out of the ground. It is surrounded by a bright-green mantle of fescue grass and mountain saxifrage, which are nurtured by the minerals that come from the water.

Down in the comparative shelter of the first valley-bottom, better soil and shelter combine to establish an ever-greater number of plants, flowers and associated food chains. The flatness of the valley-bottom permits the stream to meander for several hundred metres, and this creates pools of water in which minnows, spiders, water boatmen and freshwater shrimps set up a fine menu for visiting birds. Meadow pipits, skylarks and wagtails all nest in the surrounding area. The advantage of thicker undergrowth of grasses is that it supports a population of voles, and if we examine the edge of a pool, we can see small tunnels in the surrounding grass, with the associated piles of droppings and cut grass which indicate that this year will be a bumper one for the short-tailed vole.

The short-eared owl who nests at the edge of the heather has laid her eggs in the sure knowledge that food will be available close at hand. I hope she will share the voles with the kestrels, who, attracted for the same reason, have built their nest on a stunted rowan tree on the hillside above the stream. With luck good weather in late spring and early summer will encourage and sustain the voles as they nervously scurry about, blissfully unaware that many of them will end up in the bellies of predatory birds.

As we look upstream to the numerous little waterfalls, our eyes will be attracted to the wild thyme that clings to the sandy soil at their edges. In the late spring, in response to the early heat of the sun, the thyme produces the most wonderful flowers of pink and purple; the scent of these plants is loved by thousands of people, who purchase dried leaves of the garden variety in sachets and place them throughout their homes.

Before we leave our high glen and travel downstream to take a closer look at the valley below, it is important that we fully realise the value that the minerals in the constant water-supply provide to the majority of the things that surround us. It is the green pastures beside the stream, with their lush grass, that attract the red deer from the surrounding mountains. Just as the owls are drawn by the voles that live in the grass, so the hinds come down to find the rich food that can be turned into the mothers' milk essential to establish the next generation of deer.

With this uppermost in our minds, let us travel to the bottom of the valley, where our stream joins several others that unite to form the basis of a river. The larger water-course is perhaps only two or three metres wide, but it contains bigger stones, and pools deep enough to attract bigger fish, which migrate here in times of flood and reproduce in the autumn, laying their eggs in the redds, or underwater banks of sand and gravel.

It is here that we can see the first effects of man upon the land, as we observe how the stones have been moved and built into fanks, or enclosures, in time gone by to make holding-places for cattle and sheep. Square or rectangular fanks were designed for cattle, whereas those for sheep were round, with no corners for the animals to get stuck in. Hence one can tell from the ruins what sort of husbandry was practised in a particular place. Further over lie the remnants of an upland shieling – the small house used as temporary accommodation when farmers moved their flocks up to the summer pastures. Their sheep and cattle must have been the first creatures to change the habitats that surround this valley.

In earlier times the top of the hill, where our spring emerged, would have been covered with pine and juniper. Below that, the stream would have been completely hidden as it ran beneath the shade of a forest dominated by ash, elder, willow and birch. All those trees protected the soil from erosion, and when they were gradually removed, the richest of the soils were exposed to the elements, so that over many generations they were flushed from the mountainsides to the sea.

Fortunately, small pockets of good earth are still to be found by our stream-side, and these give us a chance to maintain some of the wildlife and plants of the original forest. Even though we have introduced pest species from foreign lands, and polluted the air and the water to such an extent that we face drastic climatic change, each and every one of us must nevertheless do everything we can to follow conservation measures that offer the best chance of survival to the wildlife that remains in the valley.

It does not matter whether we are a fortunate local resident or a passing tourist; we all have a part to play. If we take advantage of the opportunity that brought us to this riverside, and sit for a moment to meditate with an open mind, we look into the pool before us and we see young salmon swimming happily about the clear and crystal water.

This reminds us that the river is a highway which leads from the hill and glen to the distant sea, and is essential for much of the wildlife that visits far away places. The baby salmon, for example, could travel from here to Scandinavia during their lifetime. The small eels that live under the bank where we sit have just completed a fantastic journey from the Sargasso Sea, thousands of miles out in the Atlantic, and after they have grown up they will make the tremendous return journey.

Our meditation may be disturbed by the call of the ring-ouzel which sits near its nest on the cliffs above us. This visitor from Morocco has just arrived via the Straits of Gibraltar, flying up the east side of England to the River Tweed and some 50 kilometres inland, following the course of this river. The small mudslide partly hidden by the vegetation on the opposite bank was made by local otters, whose territory extends several kilometres downstream.

Our eyes may be attracted to a beautiful, small, black bird with a white chest sitting on a rock in the centre of our stream, bobbing up and down in nervous fashion as it waits to catch its morning food from the middle of the rapids. The presence of the dipper is a clear indication of the health of our mountain spring, as the bird relies on water of a good enough quality to produce the freshwater shrimps and crustaceans that are essential to its diet. When it chooses this part of the valley for its territory during the nesting season, it is a clear signal to me that our conservation measures are producing the desired results.

But we can never be complacent, for there are three main threats to the welfare of the river. One is from pollution, and we must always be aware that unwelcome chemicals from industry, farming and household waste can have a devastating effect on watercourses.

The other two dangers are inter-related – flash floods and erosion. Luckily these two can be greatly reduced by habitat management. Flash floods can completely destroy the bed of a river, as they act like a fireman's hose on the rocky foundations of the stream and remove the fine stones, sand and soil by forcing them all down towards the sea.

During the last 50 years the development of special ploughs that permit high-density hill drainage, for both farming and forestry, has had a seriously detrimental effect on upland river systems. This has now been acknowledged and, hopefully, new planning regulations will prevent drains being laid out so that they shoot rainwater directly into rivers. Unfortunately it will take many decades to minimise the damage already inflicted.

The erosion caused by bad drainage can greatly be reduced by stabilizing the stream-sides with deep-rooted grasses, rushes and shrubs such as willow planted along the banks. Vegetation can be encouraged by ensuring that daylight and sunshine reach the edge of the water so that photosynthesis can take place. Dense cover from conifers has to be avoided at all costs, as it kills ground vegetation and increases the likelihood of erosion. The natural forests that originally occupied this valley would have provided deciduous leaves for shade and cover, while at the same time producing caterpillars to enhance the food supply for wildlife in the stream. In other words, we must take every opportunity of recreating the beneficial habitat which once existed here.

We will achieve this only when we appreciate the inter-relationships of the entire valley and of the hills that surround it. We have covered only a few kilometres from the source of the river to the base of the first valley, and have considered a few inter-relationships, hopefully rekindling our enthusiasm to learn more, so that each journey we make into the countryside brings a better understanding of its wildlife, which will gradually enrich our own lives.

We need to realise, in this world of experts, that when it comes to understanding nature, there are no experts in the world of wildlife, as the inter-relationships are endless, and survival depends on the ability to readapt to the ever-changing world in which we live. Professional respect and practical experience are the best we can hope for, wherever we may wander, be it up a mountain or along a stream.

Chapter 15

HEATHER

AS heather covered the mountains and moorlands of my childhood, I grew up with a tremendous love for this wonderful, hardy plant, which has now become endangered throughout the world. It has a unique place in my heart because it produced the habitat that created the memories of those early years when I began the close association with nature which came to dominate my life. I should like to pass on some of the ideas which gradually grew in my mind as I learnt about the wildlife and habitats that we take for granted during modern times.

I can explain this best by saying that when you are a child you see things as a child, and you begin to understand the words of life. As the years go by, you sometimes are able to put words together, perhaps a sentence, then a paragraph, followed later by a chapter of the book of life, and if you are successful and diligent enough to keep an open mind, you get the wonderful experience of being able to learn from nature – the book of the countryside.

There is no better or more important message that I can put over in my limited way than to discuss the heather moors that are now in great danger of eradication. Thousands of people have gradually become aware of the problem, and would like to help restore them to their former glory. The trouble is, well-wishers often imagine that heather habitats are natural, when they are not: they do not realise that the moors will only return to their former splendour if they are intelligently managed, and if management is paid for by owners who have, in fact, been stewards of the land for generations.

If we look at a mountainside, and think of it as a jigsaw puzzle held together by different types of soil and weather, we begin to understand what we are looking at. The first thing we must appreciate is that the wildlife manager (in this case, the gamekeeper), in order to produce an annual surplus of wildlife, has developed techniques that go far beyond the beneficial management plan for red grouse. It is necessary that he maintains his heather at different heights and ages, so over the years he has perfected methods of burning different areas. This act of burning is the basis of all moorland management.

For the first few months after a patch of heather is burnt, the ground is black and bare, except for the charred stalks of the old plants. But if we return to the area one or two years later, we can witness the first vital steps in the process of overall conservation.

With dew lying early in the morning, it is possible for us to distinguish thousands of inter-related spider webs that have grown on all the short, vigorous shoots of new heather. As we look deeply into these gossamer webs, we can see the very beginnings of life. Caught in the filaments are thousands of tiny insects, which will feed grouse chicks and many other small birds in the most vulnerable part of their life, when they leave the egg and enter the dangerous world that we have created for them.

But we should also pay attention to the numerous small plants, for rich young heather is the fundamental food-source for many species, including grouse. As caterpillars return, moths and butterflies will automatically follow, and an ever-growing number of birds will also benefit as the moorland responds to management – not only the red grouse, but equally the mountain blackbird, the dunlin, the snipe and the golden plover, to name a few.

As the moor develops over the years, birds of prey such as the merlin, the peregrine and the hen harrier will all be attracted to this wonderland of wildlife. So too will carrion crows and foxes, both of which have the potential to destroy the entire system. With larger supplies of food available, active management of predators becomes all the more essential. It is up to the humans in charge to make sure that a balance is achieved, and that no particular damage is done to any one species.

So, as a wildlife manager I always find myself as judge and jury, as everything we do for conservation must ensure that the vulnerable species are protected from those which would eventually dominate the man-made habitat and, in the longer term, ensure their own destruction. The greatest danger that faces us comes from those people who think that all we have to do is remove the animals that eat heather, and the heather will return, followed by the wildlife; then everything will settle down to a wonderful, natural co-existence.

This is dangerous rubbish, because as the heather gets old its food value diminishes; the ground-cover grows long and does not allow small plants to flourish. There is abundant evidence that many of our remaining heather moors have been turned into virtual deserts by erosion, because those who own them or take the management decisions are blissfully unaware that they, themselves, are the main stumbling block to conservation.

The initial damage is quite easy to identify, as it is all too easy to see. For example, the forestry polices of the last 50 years have encouraged the planting of conifers on heather sites, which in the long term prove utterly unsuitable for growing trees. This trend was stimulated by a grant system that was in the short term beneficial to the landowner, but had dire long-term consequences for conservation. An identical situation was created by the Ministry of Agriculture when it gave grants that encouraged hill farmers to use lime dressings on heather land, and the damage was compounded by the hand-out of excessive grants for draining bogs.

All grant systems that are introduced to stimulate the redevelopment of heather should include, as an essential requirement, a long-term plan that clearly demonstrates an understanding of how to manage subsidised areas in the future. There must be a commitment not only to look after the habitat, but also to control pests and employ enough residential, full-time wildlife staff to maintain good policies indefinitely.

It is also essential that the management of surrounding areas is brought into line, for wildlife can only be re-established by creating zones large enough to accommodate all necessary species, and all the people managing the land within a zone must work in harmony.

The absence of any such policy will ensure that, instead of having wonderful, well-managed conservation heather habitats, we will merely create areas of dead scrubland that are wretched imitations of American tundra, so poor in species diversification that they cannot supply the necessary food for the large variety of wildlife found on well-managed estates from north England to north Scotland.

The threat to the future of such estates is coming from a small number of highly-motivated people whose hatred of land-ownership and field-sports is equalled only by their total failure to be able or interested enough to read the book of wildlife management. The greatest danger to our remaining moorland derives from misinformed pressure groups who, for their own reasons, favour one part of the overall picture. Unfortunately, nature cannot be stimulated by spin-doctors or misplaced subsidies managed by well-meaning people who have never actually scented the heather, heard the call of the red grouse or faced a bitter shower of rain as it sweeps across the upland moors.

Chapter 16

UPLAND RED DEER

AS my family have been connected with the management of red deer for over 200 years, I can share the pleasure and delight of the countless people who tour the Highlands and watch these beautiful animals as they graze on the mountainsides, creating precious memories for visitors from all over the world.

The sight of a large herd out in the open is sometimes taken for granted by those of us who have known it throughout our lives; but in fact the spectacle is unique, as it cannot be enjoyed in any other western country. Red deer on this scale exist nowhere else, and to see big groups of wild animals like this on bare ground, one has to go to places like Africa.

We should be grateful indeed to those who have nurtured and managed the deer, which are, after all, the impoverished descendants of much larger animals that originally lived in lowland forests. In comparatively recent times, as the trees were progressively destroyed by man, the deer were forced to move to the open mountainsides, and they had to adapt by reducing their body-weight by some 50 per cent, in order to survive on the exposed hills and in severe winter weather that their ancestors would have never faced in the warmth of their original habitat.

Poor as they are, the deer have made an immense contribution to creating the landscapes that are now synonymous with the Uplands of Scotland, and they are essential to the maintenance of the scene highly valued by visitors from all over the world. Tourist brochures and videos exploit the environment created by wildlife management, but unfortunately fail to explain in any detail how the landscape is maintained.

Imagine that we have stopped by the wayside in an isolated glen to gaze up at the open mountainsides around us. This barren landscape bears no resemblance to what has gone before, as the view, from where we sit, would not have existed four or five hundred years ago. Then, we would have been in the middle of a forest, and none of the hills would have been visible. To reach this spot, we would probably have spent several weeks on horseback or on foot – depending on how far one likes to go back in one's imagination. Man has changed this area forever, and only man can manage it for the future.

The vegetation is still dominated by heather, as this is the plant which most readily colonises acid soil. However, there are patches of green where small pockets of more fertile soil have developed, perhaps through man working the ground, or above underlying limestone. The main areas of green or light-green lie alongside the streams at the bottom of the valley – the consequence of floods washing down particles of fertile soil after the trees had been cut.

So we still have a mosaic of inter-related plants that hint at the different types of soil. The vegetation tends to be higher by the stream-side, and gradually decreases towards the top of the mountain, demonstrating how plants have been influenced by annual weather conditions and the depth of the soil.

The red deer on the mountain have made a major contribution to this habitat by their grazing – and it is the local wildlife policy and the wildlife manager, in this case the red deer stalker, who plays a vital role in ensuring that the landscape is preserved. These fragile habitats can suffer from over-grazing by sheep, cattle, hares, winter moth and deer etc. When deer damage is proven, the Deer Commission for Scotland should be involved in a habitat survey, and they should initiate and supervise a five year culling plan involving all the local estates to ensure that the deer belonging to that particular hefted area are culled without undue disturbance to neighbouring deer herds.

Many visitors mistakenly believe that the stalker is merely some sort of shooting guide for the rich. Nothing could be further from the truth, for he makes an enormous contribution to conservation in this glen. He does not work for an hourly rate; nor does he do a forty-hour week. When necessary, he works seven days a week without overtime pay or any consideration of financial gain. In fact, his dedication to this way of life is best described as a vocation.

I would not wish it to be thought that there is no rich return, for my experience has been that the greatest riches in life do not come from money. However, there is no-one naïve enough to believe that a reasonable return for one's labour is not an essential part of life.

To the uneducated eye, the deer in this glen appear to be meandering across the ground with no given pattern. In fact, a detailed understanding of their movements is vital to the conservation of both the animals and their habitat. The herd system has developed over many generations. The females dominate their own home range, while the males occupy a different area, and the two come together only for the purpose of reproduction during the rut in autumn. At all other seasons the hinds are dominated by a matriarch, who uses her experience and knowledge of the ground to lead the herd to the most suitable food, the best sanctuary, and shelter during bad weather. I have always been fascinated by these particular leading females, for their senses seem almost uncanny: if heavy snow is coming, for example, they will take their followers into a sheltered spot at least 24 hours before the blizzard strikes.

In normal weather the hinds spend most of the day high up the hillsides, where they lie digesting their food on slopes which have good visibility and are sheltered from the wind. Almost always they lie with their backs to the wind, so that they can watch the ground down-wind and rely on their acute powers of scent to warn them of any danger approaching from behind. As evening draws in, they come down off the heights to graze the good grass on the floor of the corries and glens.

Good body weight and plenty of food are vital for reproduction, and a natural mechanism ensures that if a hind is not fit enough to bear and raise a calf, her body takes a year off. She is then known as a yeld hind; but when, in another year, she does give birth, she feeds her calf as best she can by travelling to the richest feeding areas, so as to enhance her milk yield. She also introduces her offspring to the rest of the herd, so that it becomes part of the group.

A male deer, as it grows from childhood to manhood, moves from the female-dominated society to a stag group during the first two years of its life. Its nutritional requirements are slightly different, in that the ritual fighting which takes place during the rut demands that, every year, it must grow a new set of antlers. This means that it needs even more food in the spring, to produce extra calcium, and hunger often leads stags into lowland areas, where they come into conflict with forestry and farming.

As the antlers grow, covered in the furry grey skin known as velvet, they are a magnet for flies, so in early summer the stags normally move up to the tops of the mountains, where wind and weather keep insects away. They stay on the high tops for much of the summer, and return to the hinds only when the urge for reproduction races through their blood in September and October.

The rut is a time of high excitement, when big stags round up groups of hinds and calves and challenge rivals with long roars that echo across the glen. Often there are fights, which may begin with a kind of ritual parade, in which two stags walk along parallel to each other, only two or three yards apart, and then suddenly wheel inwards to lock antlers in a trial of strength. Generally a fight ends with the weaker stag giving way and moving off, but sometimes animals are wounded or even killed when one of the victor's tines (the spikes on his antlers) pierces their rib-cage. It is for this reason that stalkers always try to cull switches – stags which have no forks, but only single points, on the ends of their antlers, for such formations are most dangerous in fights.

In the Highlands the rut creates much of the revenue that is essential to the long-term prosperity of the entire habitat. Fortunately there still exist sufficient numbers of people, both male and female, who have the hunter-gatherer instinct which was once embedded in every human. These latter-day shooters are prepared to pay handsomely to take part in the annual cull, and in so doing they make an important contribution to the local economy.

Naturally, the cull must be supervised by local wildlife staff. Before going to the hill, professional stalkers, employed by the sporting estates, check that those who are going to shoot can make a safe and humane kill. Their supervision ensures that all the animals shot are part of the management plan, and their education and qualifications enable them to make certain that every animal is humanely dealt with. Prompt bleeding and gralloching (disembowelling) of carcases, and careful handling in the larder, all help to produce venison of high quality – an organic and exceptionally wholesome meat.

Yet supervision during the stag season is only one small part of the wildlife manager's duties. Another of his essential tasks is to cull the hinds and calves in winter, when daylight hours are short and the weather is often appalling. He also makes a major contribution to conservation by controlling foxes and carrion crows, without which the black grouse, the curlew, the red grouse and those rare species of the high tops, the dotterel and the ptarmigan, would all disappear.

The number of deer on the ground determines the overall annual grazing pressure, and so governs the cull. Should an estate over-shoot, the vegetation will grow high and rank, and some plants, which rely on having the habitat manicured for them, will certainly die out. Excessive disturbance by wildlife managers, through inappropriate shooting, will move the deer from their home range into surrounding regions where they will do damage to other habitats.

Many of the rarest plants, such as orchids and alpines, are maintained by deer grazing, which keeps the ground-cover at the short length they need for survival. Over-shooting may drive the deer down into farm land or forestry or, at the other end of the spectrum, push them up at the wrong time of year to the safety of the mountains, where the damage to alpine plants may be irreparable.

The overall culling plan must be tempered with a thorough understanding of the need for comprehensive management. When we see a picture of a dead stag tied on the back of a Highland pony being led off the mountain at sunset by a man clad in a local tweed, we should understand that the deer on the Garron's back was culled as part of a programme, that the man who paid to shoot it stayed at the local hotel, and that his wife probably spent a good deal of money on Scottish produce in nearby wool shops.

We should remember that the children of the professional stalker attend the local school, and that his wife and daughter probably work in the local hotel, but that the most important financial contribution to the upkeep of the valley is made by those who come to participate in field sports.

There is a place for ramblers, rock-climbers, fishers, photographers and everybody else who enjoys the great outdoors. However, careful planning will be needed to ensure that universal freedom does not result in the destruction of life in the valleys and hills. With privileges come responsibilities, whoever we may be and wherever we hail from. Informed access is good conservation. Disturbance kills.

If the deer are disturbed during times when food is scarce – for instance when snow and ice are lying in early spring – a single walker shifting a herd will cause the animals to burn more energy than they can make up by eating over the next few days. Repeated disturbance at such times will ensure that their calves suffer and eventually die a lingering death, long after the human interloper has returned to his or her centrally-heated accommodation.

Let us all share the countryside by acquiring a better understanding and respect for nature. Let us stay on the paths provided by skilled managers, which ensure that our presence does not detrimentally affect wild creatures.

As you sit down for a picnic, remember that one plastic sandwich bag will choke a young deer to death, and that a Coca Cola tin half-filled with rain becomes a death-trap for the insects that shared the heather where you sat.

Chapter 17

CHILDREN

'We do not inherit our wildlife from our parents;
we borrow it from our grandchildren.'

SOME of the most pleasant and rewarding times in my life have been spent teaching children in the Acland Centre at Eskdalemuir before a nature walk. Youngsters can be taught to understand the wonders that are abundant as they walk in a forest, with each part interdependent on each other. I know what deep enjoyment they can experience if they are instructed how to look, see, touch and smell this wonderland that so many people take for granted.

I prefer to restrict the number in any group, as this enables them to have a more personal involvement with me. Before we set out, we all sit on the floor in a semi-circle, so that facial expressions and eye-contact are enhanced, with the circle effect subconsciously relating to the cycle of life I will be suggesting. Preparation is important, for it reveals the parts of natural inter-relationships in sequence and builds up a picture in the youngsters' minds that will encourage discussion on the nature trail.

For teaching purposes I developed a large round table-top covered in green hessian that I could hang on the wall. I then placed a large picture of Eskdalemuir valley at its centre, illustrating the main land-uses and resulting habitats that influence the wildlife we would see on the walk. Forestry and sheep-farming, separated by the River Esk, formed the foundations of the landscape we would explore.

I start with a piece of rock and explain the actions of rain and frost which slowly turn it into soil. This gives me a chance to show how different rocks develop and create different types of soil, which in turn encourage and sustain different plants and present us with various colours and textures.

These in turn provide the foundations of the landscape we will be walking on.

I show how this landscape is influenced by the actions of man as he develops the habitat most suitable for his requirements, be it grassland for sheep or forest for the timber to build houses – and this is a most important point for the children to understand. I then set the scene for our walk in the wood by looking at a pine-cone and its seeds. When these drop to earth and mix with the soil we have looked at previously, the relationship between soil, seed and forest is established.

We return to the demonstration board, which has pictures set around its edge to show how each creature is dependent on another for survival. We start with the snail as a simple form of life at the bottom of the food-chain, eating soil, roots and stem material available at ground level. By showing a vole and a spider, we illustrate some of the wildlife that lives higher up the chain. We can then move on to the small bird which lives on the snail and spider, the owl that lives on the vole, and the larger birds of prey which eat the medium-sized prey available in the forest.

This pattern of life, set out on the circular board, prompts the children to think of the circular pattern of inter-relationships. This is a vital step which helps them to understand how the countryside works.

I find that the most difficult but nevertheless important part of the talk comes when we are required to discuss 'pest control'. Most of the children associate pests with cockroaches, rats, mice and wasps, which their parents have had reason to control, so I start from there and expound the reasons that justify the need to kill carrion crow, mink, fox, grey squirrel and deer – all of which, under certain circumstances, have to be restricted, as they represent a threat to the habitat or other wildlife or livestock. Just as the rat can threaten the children's home environment, so the animals I am required to control can threaten the countryside and other creatures.

I explain that there are two main reasons for pest control, one being that there is no natural habitat left in Britain, and the natural balance which existed 500 years ago no longer exists. The fundamental principle of all conservation is to create and maintain a variety of habitats, and to employ management techniques that enable the cycle of life to function freely.

Any species that reaches population-levels beyond its natural food supply can, in order to survive in the short term, switch from its natural food and damage habitats and other species that we wish to protect. So we get foxes, with no rabbits or voles to eat, killing sheep and lambs; carrion crows and magpies taking high numbers of other birds' eggs and endangering the survival of rare species. In the absence of the wolf, all species of deer need to be culled by humans.

Introduced species, which have no natural food supply in our countryside, present us with special problems – for instance, grey squirrels, which were brought over from America in the 19th century, and mink, which are designed to live in Canada but not here, are both a major threat to many British birds and animals. Sika deer from China and flat worms from New Zealand are further introductions which cause major damage to our countryside and require culling.

Young children have no difficulty in accepting the need for pest control. The idea of culling surplus predators does not worry them. It is only later in their lives that teachers start to change their opinions, and as they grow older they are influenced more and more by the media.

I find it important that children should see the countryside as a jigsaw puzzle, and wildlife management as a means of filling-in the pieces we have lost, so that we can maintain and improve the picture to its fullest potential, thus ensuring that future human generations will inherit the results. It should always be remembered that we borrow our flora and fauna from the children, and do not inherit from our fathers. If we destroy them by ignorance or greed, we have failed.

I emphasise that conservation means giving nature a helping hand. Examples at Eskdalemuir are the dramatic increases in badgers, deer, hedgehogs and red squirrels, all in response to the creation of new habitats within the forest and the management policies employed by the staff. The last photograph on my lecture board illustrates a dead rabbit being eaten by beetles beside a toadstool. This marks the end of the cycle – the recycling of wildlife in the form of animal and bird, and the beginning of new life, starting from the decomposing material of the beetles created by death as we see it. We have now followed the story from birth to death.

As I have spent most of my life in the forest, and have happy memories of my own childhood, and also enjoy the priceless gift of a family of my own, I find I can communicate with the children, using the experience I shared with my own offspring. My background gives me the confidence to share with visiting youngsters and their teachers the sights and tracks that stimulate their curiosity and thirst for answers as they observe the wildlife surrounding them along the trail.

From the start of the walk, it is important that gentle but firm supervision is established, for the safety of the pupils and the good of the class as a whole. My experience of children from a variety of countries leads me to conclude that they all carry on much the same, according to the average age. This means that one can predict their general behaviour patterns, and avoid possible problems along the way by fitting the particular nature trail to the age group.

A normal class falls into three sections. There are the forward runners, who need to be restrained for their own safety; then come the main group, who usually walk hand in hand, with chosen friends as an extra form of security as they enter the new forest experience. These children only require reassurance and encouragement to get them interested in the wildlife around them, and they are soon full of questions, having a happy and memorable time. Last but not least comes the small number of less motivated and less able pupils who require special attention and encouragement. I usually find that they have a particular interest in flowers or bright colours, and this can be encouraged to bring them into the mainstream of the safari.

The progress of the party must be dictated by this last group. If they are relaxed, they soon become involved with the subjects they are interested in, whether these be flowers, tracks, birds, animals or the general debris they pick up from the forest floor. Such finds usually prompt many questions, especially if they find an old bone or skeleton.

Very soon the forward scouts of the group, hurrying back and forth on the start of the trail and finding little of interest, run out of steam and settle down to enjoy the rest of the walk, so that we all become a united party. When this takes place, I lead them to various points of interest and subjects that will stimulate them to ask relevant questions, as they subconsciously begin to read the forest environment and reap the benefits, particularly if they are encouraged to touch things and discover some interesting object, even though I have carefully led them to it.

Fortunately, the local roe deer always make use of the path which we walk, and this offers me a perfect opportunity to show the children how they mark out their boundaries by rubbing trees and scraping their scent on the ground to establish their own territories. We can also see how they use the willow and cotoneaster I planted for them to rub velvet from their antlers each year: we find their sleeping-places, and from the bed-marks tell how many are in the family group.

I am always looking for examples that will encourage the children to think positively about their countryside, and I have been much encouraged by their ability to grasp the fundamental principles of what I tell them in the forest. When we see a kestrel hovering above us, I ask what bird it is, and someone always has the right answer. I can then ask why it is there, and get the response that it is looking for food – so then we discuss what that will be, and I am told a vole or beetle. Both are to be found on the grass meadow where we stand, and I explain that the meadows were left open for the deer and their management.

We can then go on to discuss why the area was chosen, and understand it was for its soil, so we are back at a practical demonstration of the first lesson in the morning.

Hopefully, my little flock now view their surroundings in a different way, and see the kestrel as part of the cycle of life, not as an isolated object. It is hovering there for the vole which is in the grass, and the vole is there because the grass is growing on the right type of soil, and the soil originated from rock, which made it rich, and as this habitat grows the food favoured by the deer, we left it unplanted. All parts of the observation fit together. Here endeth the first lesson, with many more on interdependence along the way.

Some of my most treasured letters, many with drawings, come from children with whom I have spent the day. Although I get the general format dictated by the teacher, their own impressions of the outing shine through as they add their own highlights of the walk. They are not usually impressed by rarities we have seen: rather, they are interested in common things that appeal to them, such as a roe deer bed, a scent-mark on a willow, a group of tadpoles in the pond, or a toad we disturbed taking shelter under a stone. Even things such as a dead frog I showed them which had been killed by a heron; one little boy decided to put it in his jacket pocket to show his mother. I hope she was suitably impressed. The most valuable point to me was the chance of demonstrating to the children the relationship between the frog in the pond and the heron that killed it: pond habitat for frog, food for the heron, life and death.

That was one good, memorable example of the fact that the countryside is not the world of Alice in Wonderland or of Beatrix Potter. Animals and birds do not love or look after each other in the way that humans do. The reality is predator and prey, survival and death, and to teach children any other message is dangerous nonsense, of the kind often seen on television.

When Mr. Hedgehog is 'saved' by some well meaning do-gooder, taken to the vet and returned to the wild, its enemies will not help look after it, but will welcome the fact that it has been injured, as that will make it vulnerable, and all the easier for them to kill and eat. Such rescue work is not conservation, although it provides emotional viewing. It is certainly part of conservation to give nature a helping hand and respect all wildlife, but we should fully understand what happens to animals when they are returned to the countryside. Starvation, isolation and a slow death are the normal reality – but such a progression would not make good TV, so it is avoided at all costs, resulting in a completely untrue presentation of what takes place in the wild wood.

Let us endeavour to tell our children the truth about the countryside so that perhaps they will look after it better than we are doing. I regard education as a vital part of conservation, and it is essential that town and country live in harmony. Hopefully my work in the Acland Wildlife Centre was a small step in that direction. Sadly, after I retired, there were some people high up in the company who did not share my views on comprehensive wildlife management, and in 1996 the Centre was closed – on one of the saddest days of my life. Subsequently the site has been sold for private housing.

Fortunately, many of the forest blocks at Eskdalemuir have been recently purchased by two Austrians who understand and value wildlife management as an essential part of woodland ownership. They, together with a number of other owners, enabled my son Ronald to set up his own wildlife management company to look after their properties, and he built the Fingland Training Centre in Eskdalemuir, where we have the pleasure of training students from all over the world in forest design and conservation management. We get great pleasure and satisfaction from passing on our experiences to the next generation and sharing information with fellow professionals.

Chapter 18

INTO THE FUTURE

IN April 2003, sitting beside a freshwater spring which we had found high up on the western edge of Blackhouse, I could see across the hills of the Southern Uplands of Scotland to the Lake District. The water was wonderfully fresh and clear as it bubbled out of the hillside, and I drank a cup of it with David Beevers to celebrate what we had achieved. Behind me stood a hut that I built as a place from which to observe the wildlife on the moors above the tree-line.

I had decided that it was time for me to retire from full-time wildlife management. 'Time waits for no one'. I would hand responsibility for the area into the capable hands of my son, and become a keenly-interested observer. My mind went back over all my time in the Uplands of Scotland. I remembered my childhood, and the years I spent learning to know and love them, and the wildlife that inhabits them. I remembered too my arrival at Eskdalemuir and the challenges involved in persuading the forestry world to accept my ideas.

My memories moved on to my work at Blackhouse. How much the landscape here had changed, and how much had been achieved! I thought of the development of the forest and woodland, the building of the ponds, the opening-up of the valley-sides, the broad-leaf planting, and everything else that we did to create an ideal habitat for black grouse and the other wildlife that has developed.

So much for my hillside reverie. My main task now is to act as a consultant and liaison officer on wildlife matters and forest design, in which I am still heavily involved. I have produced wildlife management plans for estates as disparate as Chatsworth in Derbyshire, and Balmoral on Deeside, and the fact that I have won several leading wildlife awards for my work ranging from blackgame to deer, and also the Fred Courtier award for "outstanding contribution to wildlife management" shows, I hope, that my record in these matters is sound. The grant of a Winston Churchill fellowship enabled me to make a detailed study of wildlife management and habitat establishment in Scandinavia, Holland and Germany.

At the time of writing, I am serving on various national committees, and also advise the Scottish Gamekeepers Association on wildlife policy. This means that I sit on specialist panels at the Scottish Parliament, where I do everything possible to lay accurate information about the countryside before MSPs, so that they at least have sound facts based on practical experience – rather than whimsical theories – on which to base decisions. Probably my most important role over the past two years has been as a member of the Select Committee set up to formulate the best practices for the management of Scotland's deer – a body which has been extremely well received and will become very influential.

I am the Senior Lecturer at the Acland Training Centre at Eskdalemuir, which is run by my son Ronald. There we teach all Highland College graduates, police wildlife officers and other delegations interested in wildlife and forest conservation. We also act as assessors and teachers of candidates for the Deer Stalking Certificate Levels 1 & 2 – professional managers come from all over Britain and Europe, some from as far away as Italy. Part of this tuition takes place on the ground, on large estates.

In other words, I am still actively engaged in wildlife matters – but the outlook, far from being rosy, is worrying, for in spite of all that has been done, Scotland's countryside is faced by numerous threats, not least from large organisations who control more and more of our countryside environment.

I am of the firm opinion that some policy-makers, rather than the staff "on the ground", are adopting unsound policies, thus misrepresenting the case for practically applied wildlife conservation and management. These policies, if implemented, will in my opinion have a seriously negative effect on the environment and therefore the wildlife.

I would submit that some of these organisations, because of their dependence on membership numbers, are continually faced with a dilemma: either they support the need for balanced pest control and thus risk alienating a substantial number of members, or they supply their members with incomplete information. I am personally not concerned with problems of the relationship with their members; what does concern me is the tendency to adopt management policies which are influenced by membership figures rather than what is best for the wildlife. Birds of prey are often predominant in member's minds, and excessive numbers of raptors in some parts of the British Isles can – and often do – cause serious problems which these organisations are reluctant to address. They also tend to over-prioritise the occasional – nevertheless inexcusable – killing of a bird of prey by rural dwellers. These isolated instances are presumably good media coverage for the recruitment of yet more members.

There are many instances of wrongly motivated mismanagement, but here I select just four examples, to show how acutely things can go wrong.

1. Moorland Madness

A few miles east of Eskdalemuir lies Langholm, once a 5,000-hectare expanse area of rare heather moorland which had been nurtured and maintained by generations of gamekeepers on behalf of the Duke of Buccleuch's family – owners dedicated to good stewardship of the land for centuries. The moor, which extends from the town of Langholm to Newcastleton was so well managed that each year, a large surplus of red grouse could be harvested.

To produce game on this scale, the moorland keeper must sensitively control the predators which could otherwise destroy the grouse and their eggs, so that he can create the surplus stock which allows shooting to take place. This in turn provides the money to pay the wages of wildlife staff and other expenses – houses, vehicles and equipment. The point which many conservationists cannot or will not accept is that by controlling – not eliminating – foxes, stoats, mink, crows, magpies etc., the keepers not only preserve the grouse, but also create a surplus of plover, curlew, redshank, black grouse and other upland birds, so that the conservation value of their work is of the highest order.

In 1992 the Duke of Buccleuch gave permission for a five-year experiment, designed to determine once and for all the impact of hen harriers on grouse. Under the auspices of Scottish Natural Heritage, a joint team from the Game Conservancy Trust and the Institute of Terrestrial Ecology monitored the hen harriers' nesting at Langholm, and one of the bodies funding the work was the RSPB. Some conservationists sent all sorts of wonderful expressions spinning around – 'ecological balance', 'over-balance' and 'natural predation' were freely invoked, but they were reluctant to listen to experienced wildlife managers, who were convinced that eventually the raptors themselves would ruin their own environment.

This is precisely what happened. Close surveillance of nest-sites revealed that the hen harriers, left unchecked, had a disastrous effect on the moor and killed a high proportion of all the moorland species throughout the year. The number of raptors rose to twenty-eight nesting pairs, and they had a lethal impact not only on the grouse but also on most of the other moorland birds. In five years the annual grouse harvest fell from several thousand to 100. Shooting became unviable, so the income dried up. Parties of well-shod shooting people ceased visiting Langholm; thus their money was no longer spent in local shops and hostelries. All five gamekeepers had to be stood down, and four of them lost their jobs. Regular heather-burning ceased. A scheme proposed by the Game Conservancy, whereby eggs would be taken under licence from harrier nests and hatched in incubators, so that chicks could be reared in captivity and set free in other areas, was shunned by the RSPB. Attempts at artificially feeding the raptors with dead rats and chicks proved ineffective. The harriers eventually filtered away because they had eaten themselves out of house and home, and the moor turned into a virtual wildlife desert.

Since then the former head keeper, Brian Mitchell, has continued to burn some of the heather, to keep it going in the hope that more realistic policies will be adopted, and also to cull foxes, for the benefit of local sheep farmers. A few sheep browse on the sitka spruce that have regenerated naturally, but there is scarcely a wild creature to be seen, apart from a few carrion crows hunting the moor from end to end. In 2003 the scientific group studying the area reported that the moor was supporting one pair of harriers, which produced only two chicks.

When the Buccleuch Estates proposed to salvage something from the ruins by planting Scots pine and native broad-leaves on parts of the moor, their plan and request for a grant was rejected by the Forestry Commission, on the grounds that one of the plantations would be within two kilometres of a harrier nest-site, and the birds might be disturbed. My own experience – practical experience combined with detailed observation – shows that forestry operations can be carried out within a few hundred metres of nests without causing the harriers any anxiety.

Perhaps it is time for us to persuade the authorities that, when conservation and other bodies receive large grants and subsidies to purchase tracts of land for the purpose of protecting rare or threatened species, an independent wildlife audit should be made of any property they propose to manage. Then five years later an assessment should be made of their success or failure – and also at the end of a ten year span. There could be penalty clauses, whereby Government grants become repayable, should conservation measures prove to have failed, and wildlife to have declined rather than increased.

I have no doubt that at Langholm, if Brian Mitchell and a team of keepers were reinstated, the heather and the moorland birds could be re-established within ten years, perhaps within five. Such a development would, I hope, furnish the proof that sporting estates in the main are first rate practitioners of conservation.

My own experience suggests that three or four pairs of hen harriers could nest at Langholm every year without any detriment to the shooting programme, and that the other moorland birds would return in force if a team of gamekeepers selectively controlled the major predators. But – and this is the crucial point – to achieve a viable balance, the wildlife managers would have to be issued with licences authorising them to control agreed numbers of raptors – perhaps by removing some of their eggs, which could be hatched elsewhere – unfortunately this is something which the RSPB is unlikely to condone.

2. Capercaillie and Black Grouse.

Over the past few years one of the most agitated disputes among conservationists has concerned capercaillie, the magnificent woodland gamebird, the largest grouse in the world. The population of this fine bird is falling in Britain, and is reckoned to be down to 1,000 at the most. The bird purists maintain that the caper's decline has been mainly due to fatal collisions with the six-foot-high fences built to keep deer out of young plantations, into which the birds fly, particularly at dawn and dusk.

This conclusion is based largely on a single study carried out between 1989 and 1995, during which fourteen birds were supposedly killed on fences at one location. The study failed to analyse several related factors, among them the design and alignment of the fences, the lay-out of the forest, disturbance by humans, and so on. Working from this one dubious statistic, the 'green' organisations advocate that all deer fences should be removed from capercaillie woodlands, and that the only way to regenerate Scotland's forests is to eliminate the deer – both red, sika and roe – within the woodlands and the surrounding areas.

The idea that deer-fences are the big grouse's main problem is, in my opinion, totally wrong. Wire barriers do undoubtedly kill a small number of them. The most worrying demise of blackgame has occurred in Wales, Northern England and the south of Scotland, where there are practically no deer fences. The main reasons for both caper and black grouse decline are the loss of suitable habitat, bad weather in early summer, and above all predation.

When I started work for the Forestry Commission in 1951, capercaillie and black grouse were at their highest population levels, with the caper population alone estimated at 20,000. My first task was to tie bunches of heather and wine-bottle corks to deer fences, to make the wire mesh more visible, and this simple precaution proved most effective. It is interesting to note that the people who advocated the removal of fences are now receiving substantial Government grants so that they can study various types of fence design – research which is completely unnecessary.

I spent some twenty years looking after the caper in the core area of Loch Lomond National Park. During that time their numbers increased, with many birds choosing young commercial plantations as suitable nesting habitat. The area was criss-crossed by deer fences – yet during those twenty years I never had a single casualty caused by impact with the wire. Moreover, the carefully-managed herd of deer within my beat made a major contribution to the maintenance of the habitat that the woodland grouse prefer. I learned that good forest edge is all-important to caper, as are open areas of grass for the supply of insects. Blaeberry is also a vital source of food, and larch trees provide safe roost. In stark contrast, I became involved in a study of caper in an area where there was no effective control of predators, and in one year five out of six nests under observation were destroyed by carrion crows and foxes. It is foxes, not fences, that need to be removed.

Fences are an important element in woodland management, and essential for the regeneration of Scots pine – the trees on which caper depend for their food in winter. Seedlings cannot grow to maturity without protection, and especially while a new plantation is becoming established, protection is essential – otherwise the deer browse off the saplings, stunting or killing them. That said, it is important that fences should be intelligently positioned and aligned, if possible in gullies, and there should always be a screen of young trees or bushes to lift airborne birds over them.

To remove all the deer from the area is not the answer, for the long-term welfare of the birds will depend on the vegetation being controlled by a reasonable number of deer. Success can only be achieved by correct selection of tree-species and an enlightened approach. Everything is a matter of balance: the structure of the forest is constantly changing, and it must be shaped by professionals who understand the requirements of the wildlife in the area.

Elsewhere in northern Europe, caper are also declining, but at a far less alarming rate. In Sweden alone the annual harvest – harvest, not population – is estimated to be about 25,000 birds. In all, the annual surplus in Sweden, Norway and Finland amounts to double this figure, produced by positive management of the habitat, and effective predator control.

The Scandinavian capercaillie thrive in large conifer forests, which in some areas extend to 80 per cent of the land area. They are managed so that there are always plenty of young pine and birch trees throughout the woodland cover. Forest edge, bog-land, moorland with blaeberry, and old pines for roosting are all taken into account in the design and management plan; they combine to form ideal caper habitat, enabling the birds to rear good broods of chicks every year. Predator control is given high priority, and this ensures that the eggs and chicks are not eaten by foxes, crows, pine martens and goshawks, all of which have been identified as threats to the woodland grouse's survival. Not identified as a threat are the many kilometres of two-metre high fences built to control the movements of elk, around the forests and through them: reports of caper being involved in lethal collisions with wire are scarce.

Where does this leave Scotland's beleaguered population, which has been reduced to the brink of extinction by bad weather and negative pest control? Large areas of the country are now covered in young commercial forests, which could provide ideal habitat, like that of Scandinavia. Why, then, have we got such a problem?

When the Scottish Parliament was charged by Brussels to look after the capercaillie and reinstate the species, it set up a Capercaillie Biodiversity Action Plan Steering Group – a grand title indeed! Many members were drawn from Government departments which had negative policies on predator control. A significant proportion of the Steering Group lacked practical experience of wildlife management, and from the start the body was seriously flawed, because its members were unable to face up to the obvious necessity to control specific predators – including the goshawk and pine marten. Despite scientific studies and experienced wildlife managers having established that these two species represent a major threat to

Scotland's capercaillie, this body appears to avoid these facts when liaising with the Scottish Executive.

The Group has spent great amounts of taxpayers' money on projects such as the removal of many kilometres of deer fences, in the erroneous belief that the barriers were somehow responsible for the birds' decline. They also identified snaring – one important method of fox-control, especially in areas which are unsuitable for spot-lighting – as a major danger to woodland grouse; when in fact all that is needed is a stop on each wire, to prevent birds being caught.

There is now a serious dilemma. Politicians and scientists do not like to admit mistakes, even when decisions turn out to have been based on faulty information. In this case, some members of the Steering Group now admit that goshawks and pine martens 'may' be a threat to the caper, and are suggesting that scientific research should be commissioned to discover the facts. I feel that this is an unnecessary delaying factor, and a waste of valuable time and money. Most wildlife managers, both here and in Scandinavia, have known for many years that these particular predators can kill 80 per cent of nesting birds and young.

I can only hope that wiser counsel will emanate from the Scottish Executive, and that this unfortunate state of affairs is addressed. I also hope that experienced wildlife managers are appointed to the Group in sufficient numbers to bring about a balanced adjustment of policies. No further funds should be spent on unnecessary research into predation or deer fencing when there is already overwhelming evidence to justify the immediate establishment of effective pest-control, before the caper population falls to a level from which it can not recover.

It is no surprise to find that most of the the core-areas identified for the survival of British capercaillie were brought into their fine condition mainly by sporting estates in the Central and North-east Highlands of Scotland. Few, if any, of the tourists who enjoy the Highland scenery realise that such traditional estates, far from making a profit, are often run at a loss, and cost sizeable sums every year to maintain. It is the owners' interest in shooting, stalking and fishing, and the pleasure they derive from land stewardship, that keep upland habitats in good order. If pressure groups – motivated by factors other than the future welfare of wildlife – drive out these landowners, they will destroy our priceless rural heritage.

3. **Lament for Creag Meagaidh.**

I'm truly sorry man's dominion
Has broken Nature's social union,
An justifies that ill opinion,
Which makes thee startle
At me, thy poor, earth-born companion,
An fellow mortal!

Robert Burns.

My brother David was Nature Conservancy Council Warden for the eastern Cairngorm area from 1962 to 1979. The Conservancy staff at this time consisted of a majority of experienced wildlife managers who were informed conservationists. It was when they were amalgamated into Scottish Natural Heritage that the rot set in. Scotland's wildlife heritage is being endangered by numbers of post-graduates with doctorates, whose practical experience of wildlife management does not extend beyond the window boxes of suburbia.

In 1983 the Creag Meagaidh estate, in Glen Spean, east of Fort William – one of the most beautiful parts of Scotland – was put up for sale by Loch Laggan Estates. A client for whom we were acting at Eskdalemuir showed interest, so I went to check the place out; but after a careful inspection of the land, which extends to almost 4,000 hectares, I submitted a report saying that the estate, a typical red deer forest of the kind on which I myself had grown up, would be permanently damaged by an investment in conifer woodlands on the scale envisaged. In the event, the area was bought by another commercial company, Fountain Forestry, and then in 1985 by the Nature Conservancy Council, predecessor of Scottish Natural Heritage, which paid £441,000 – taxpayers' money, of course. The estate became the Creag Meagaidh National Nature Reserve, and offered an opportunity to show that State ownership could in fact promote policies that would maintain Scotland's wildlife for the future, by working in harmony with the surrounding estates which had been practising effective management for generations.

It was therefore with deep sadness that when I returned to Creag Meagaidh in 2002, the abundance wildlife I had seen during my first visit had been severely reduced. I knew at once there was something drastically wrong, and that there had been gross mismanagement. The food chain had been broken, ensuring there were no birds of prey – none of the eagles, kestrels or short-eared owls that I had recorded during my first visit. There was also a distinct absence of other birds. Even the orchids which I had admired during my first visit were buried under a carpet of uneaten vegetation.

As this habitat does not maintain young blaeberry or heather – vital to the local black game population, these birds will gradually disappear. A small number of cocks will return from the neighbouring sporting estates to "lek", but the absence of suitable food will ensure that the greyhens will emigrate to take advantage of the better management policies taking place around this "nature reserve". The general public, attracted to this area by the surrounding landscapes, are not impressed when they find the dead heather and uneaten vegetation that precedes birchwood scrub establishment. Between 1992 and 1999, the visitor numbers have dropped continually, and the majority of visitors who use this area are either on their way up the path to "bag a Monroe", or to go ice climbing in the winter as they have done for generations. SNH's glossy hand-outs, whose cover picture shows the magnificence of Creag Meagaidh when it was a red deer forest estate, bears no resemblance to the landscape that will develop if this subsidised misman-agement is permitted to continue.

In 2002 Scottish Natural Heritage produced a report on this reserve which makes interesting reading. The reserve's accounts show that it is making a significant annual loss, which of course has to be born by the tax payer. However, one paragraph buried in the middle of this report – for 1997 to 2000 – reveals that neither the running costs of this estate, nor payments of capital cost, depreciation, or even annual salaries are included in the figures. Ninety percent of the income comes from red deer stalking, yet the stated policy is to kill most of them, in order to create an unfenced birchwood area. I only wish that I too could have lived in this land of the cloud-cuckoo when I had to justify the cost of conservation to an owner.

One report claims that in 1992 the estate had almost eliminated the deer, and that this had not affected the surrounding estates. How can this be? SNH's own accounts clearly demonstrate: ten years later, they are still making £10,000 a year from sales of venison. If they have no deer of their own, where are all their carcases coming from? Furthermore, it has been clearly stated by the Chairman of the Monadhliath Deer Management Group – Jamie Williamson – that 'surrounding estates experienced reduced red deer numbers as a result of the Creag Meagaidh cull when compared to elsewhere in the deer group area'. Any qualified and experienced person could have predicted this sorry state of affairs which will only escalate as this scrubland develops and the local red and roe deer are attracted to this vacuum area. If further proof was needed, it has been admitted by SNH staff themselves that they have been forced to apply to the Deer Commission for Scotland for night shooting permission – to kill deer at night as they enter from the surrounding estates.

As this is a top tourist area, the report on the effects of this reserves' negative contribution to the local economy should have stated the following facts: The revenue from one hill-walker is estimated at between £5 and £10 per day, as the vast majority will bring their own packed lunch, and fuel their vehicle at home before they start. A visiting deer-stalker, in contrast, contributes from £480 to £500 a day, not counting whatever his wife spends in local wool mills, shops and hotels. A grouse shooter is reckoned to be worth over £500 a day. Driven birds are charged at a rate of £115 per brace, so a 100 brace day brings in over £11,000.

There is a clear need for an independent assessment of the workings of this estate, because the questionable information coming from it is now spreading like a cancer through the uplands of Scotland; particularly when evidence is taken with regard to management policies within our national parks for the future. When it is realised that land-use of this kind imposes a huge burden on the tax-payer, and destroys the wildlife of the country, it is time for a thorough inquiry into the policies being advocated by a small number of activists. The beauty of Glen Spean was created by the long-term stewardship of the sporting estates; and the splendid background scenery in the television series "Monarchs of the Glen" was filmed on one of them. Maybe another TV series should be made, this time of the recent innovations at Creag Meagaidh, and given the name of that other popular favourite, "Neighbours from Hell".

The Deer for Commission Scotland – formerly the Red Deer Commission – is the Government body responsible for the welfare and sustainable management of Scotland's deer. I have always supported its executives in their important and difficult task, but unfortunately I have found that a small proportion of the delegates who sit on its committees, and seek to influence policy, have minimal practical knowledge or experience. Rather than make sensible recommendations, there are signs that they are pursuing agendas based on questionable data and swayed by political considerations. This results in pressure being applied to other delegates, who, even though they lack practical experience, are honestly attempting to make decisions in the long-term interest of our wildlife heritage.

Over the years I have heard countless misleading statements made which can and do influence the general public. The first such pronouncement is always that there are too many red deer in Scotland. This is a misleading generality, and is usually followed by some "guestimate" of the overall population: the statistics rolled out vary from time to time by hundreds of thousands, depending on which expert is holding forth, and the figures are then fed, with great effect, to the media. As there is no way of arriving at a really accurate figure for the deer population, the vague assessments given out are counter-productive to good management.

Deer numbers are no longer accepted as the best yardstick by which to assess the impact the animals make on their environment. The only way forward is to measure accurately the damage to commercial forest crops and other upland habitats. Plans for future management will only be sound if field staff are trained to monitor the habitat and identify accurately the various types of damage being inflicted on the environment in any specific area.

My own forest studies clearly demonstrate that over 50 per cent of all the complaints levelled at deer have nothing to do with deer whatsoever. Deer should not be blamed for over-grazing by domestic stock such as sheep, cattle and occasionally goats. Damage can result from the activities of voles, beetles, and from unenlightened forest policies – chiefly the managers' failure to consult soil maps, and to match both conifers and broad-leaves with suitable soil-types. Trees which are genetically unsuitable to local climates and which are not "site-native" will never thrive, especially if they are planted by unsupervised contractors.

The public is now very keen on the regeneration of woodlands, broad-leaves in particular, and all manner of carefully selected information and data is disseminated on this subject. Favourable comparisons are made with Continental practice, but these are fundamentally flawed. Scotland's natural woodlands have been cleared by man, with the result that in many areas no sources of native seeds remain, and over the centuries the soil has become too degraded to grow the full complexity of native tree species which once grew there. On the continent, the traditions of forest and deer management reach back much farther: good husbandry has ensured that soils are more fertile, and seed sources more abundant. It is simply not true that deer-densities are lower on the Continent than here – on many European estates roe deer populations are far higher than in many areas of Scotland.

Another destructive feature is that ill-considered culling is driving deer from the grounds which they have used for generations. Pushed on and on by relentless killing, the survivors are seeking refuge on the high tops, among the rocks and alpine flora. The result is that misconceived shooting policies, aimed at reducing grazing pressure, have been completely counter-productive; a clear case of self-inflicted injury.

One of the more negative and dangerous attacks on deer management was made by ill-informed activists during the 1990s, when they managed to convince the Scottish Government that the reduction in blackgame and capercaillie was due mainly to the prevalence of deer-fences. I have already demonstrated the inaccuracy of this claim. Nevertheless, the idea that deer fences were a menace took hold, and was energetically promoted in the media, masking the fact that the real threat to woodland grouse comes from predators and habitat loss. The result was that landowners began to dismantle fences, thereby greatly escalating deer damage in young woodlands, increasing the risk of accidents on roads, and facilitating the indiscriminate massacre of hundreds of animals which came down off the hill to feed on lowland farms and grouse moors, and are mown down on open ground, where riflemen can surround them.

Another reason put forward by inexperienced conservationists for slaughtering deer is the claim that they destroy precious alpine flora. The truth is that the damage caused in alpine or semi-alpine zones is done almost entirely by sheep, hares and winter moth. Delegates to conferences often avoid any reference to the magisterial report on deer management produced by Paul van Vlissingen, owner of the 40,000-hectare Letterewe Estate – "A Highland Deer Herd and its Habitat". Published in 2002, this gives a clear and detailed account of continuous scientific studies carried out on Letterewe over a three-year period. These showed that the resident deer herd makes a major contribution not only to the local economy, but also to the health of the habitat, because their selective grazing allows the alpine flora to flourish. The report concluded that the removal of deer, far from improving the environment, would threaten the biodiversity of the entire area; a fact that has been very recently supported by an independent study on the Isle of Rum.

Glenfeshie

My father always told me that the road to hell was paved with good intentions, and the sad plight of Scotland's red deer is no exception. As the activists follow their misguided attempt to recreate an upland countryside that is unachievable and unsustainable, thousands of deer are killed through their political manipulation, and their rhetoric bears no resemblance to the truth. Words like "culling" are used instead of killing; "selective management" meaning mindless slaughter, are fed to the general public, whose members in most cases only have a very shallow knowledge of woodland and wildlife management, and in many cases none whatsoever.

I now ask you to join me on a ringside seat of reality, to see what is actually taking place throughout the Highlands. You join me at daybreak on a February morning, 2004, on a remote hillside far from the MSPs in Edinburgh, or the misinformed general public, many of whom are members of the very organisations which are demanding the killing of deer that live in this locality. There are hundreds of red deer, clearly distressed as they have been harried and hounded into this pathetic and exposed herd – to face death. The morning stillness in this remote Glen of Feshie – where Landseer painted that wonderful picture of "A Stag at Bay" – is a mockery of what will take place today as a government sponsored helicopter shatters the peace and tranquillity, as it ferries out a group of contract killers and lands them on the surrounding hillside. The helicopter then turns and herds the terrified deer toward the waiting killers, and the bloodbath begins, with only the lucky ones dying humanely. Many will be wounded, traumatised, and terrified while the motherless young that escape will die a long and lingering death in some remote peat bog. The indiscriminate killing of the matriarch females within the group will destabilise and destroy the established herd system which has evolved through the millennia, and which is essential to their welfare and management.

This nightmare scenario is committed by government employees, and the removal of the deer fencing, which has ultimately led to this carnage, was sponsored by the public purse. Obviously a change in the law is urgently required, but more importantly we need to realise as a nation that it is not Scotland's deer that are the problem, it is the mindless minority who manipulate the media and misinform our politicians.

The Way Ahead

As I have demonstrated, the countryside will always be an unnatural habitat, in which conservation of flora and fauna will demand active management to maintain a balance beneficial to the welfare of the most endangered species. My work on the Blackhouse estate was but one example. Red deer forests and heather moorland for red grouse are two other prime candidates for conservation. Golden plover, curlew, ptarmigan, golden eagle and other rare species all depend on those habitats and their management for their survival.

The greatest threat to conservation in areas such as Eskdalemuir and Blackhouse is disturbance. Fortunately both places are remote and far from the public view. At the same time, it is important for educational purposes that conservation activities are brought to the attention of as many people as possible. The video camera that I have carried for years has given thousands of people a sight of what I talk about without the wildlife being stressed by hordes of visitors, and I think that in future greater use of cameras will be vital for conservation work.

But participation, although it has to be carefully controlled, is also an important part of the learning process. One-day visits for organisations such as the Scottish Falconry Club, two days' grouse shooting for the German Pointer Trials, visits from field officers of the RSPB, the Countryside Rangers' Service and the Tweed Authority, plus many other deputations, have all served to put over a positive message to those involved in upland wildlife re-generation.

We, in return, have gained greatly from discussions with fellow professionals, with the result that we can all move forward together by exchanging experiences and adapting ideas to formulate future plans.

I hope that the designs developed at Blackhouse will help other interested estate owners with their own conservation plans. Large areas of the hillside that were originally planted with larch and sitka spruce have now been thinned to allow the vegetation to re-establish itself beneath them. The sunlight, penetrating through to the ground, has encouraged the blaeberry and heather to grow again, and the buds of the larch are appreciated by the birds in the springtime.

The large valley-bottoms which we left open for the greyhens are also very attractive to foxes intent on predation. Here the observation points we built have become just as important for the control of foxes as the boxes and towers we put up to enable us to control deer, particularly sika. Our policy of culling foxes hard in all the blackcock sites is very important. Throughout the development we have taken all legal means of controlling mink, crows and the small number of grey squirrels that frequent the area.

So what do I see for the future? First, since Blackhouse and its habitat are closely associated with development of the forest edge, I was delighted to read details of the new Scottish Forestry Grant System, published in January 2003, as it presents a fantastic opportunity to establish true bio-diversity woodlands, and appears to offer real incentives to the responsible land-owners of the future. But our education will have to move even further if we are to maintain the habitats that this scheme will encourage.

In the past, full-time wildlife staff have been paid for mainly by land-owners at their own expense. In future, payment by Government bodies could well be of great importance. This should become a national responsibility, and be covered under the grant scheme.

The thorny problem of managing some birds of prey will also have to be addressed. As the Blackhouse project developed from its early stages, I was delighted to witness the arrival of the hen harrier, the merlin, the buzzard and the peregrine, which have all nested in the area and brought up young annually, boosted by the surplus food which improvement of the habitat produced. Unfortunately, however, the overall population of some birds of prey, in particular the goshawk, has now become a threat in places such as this, where a rare and rapidly declining species – the black grouse – faces the prospect of elimination. In 2003, for the first time, I witnessed extensive disturbance and damage at several of the lekking areas.

It would appear that the killing and overall disturbance at the leks is the work of a relatively small number of rogue birds, but the damage they have inflicted is very serious. If the blackcock are driven from the their breeding grounds, the whole reproductive system will break down and the species will rapidly disappear.

It is our duty to look after the habitats that support the animals of the forest and the mountain, the fish of the waters and the birds of the air, as none of these creatures belong to us. We may have inherited them from our parents and grandparents, but we are, above all, borrowing them from our grandchildren.

The misinformed 'experts' who claim that upland areas can be turned into important nature reserves without realistic management are a menace to Scotland's wildlife. Far from thriving, most of the birds and animals that once flourished there will inevitably disappear as a consequence of negative policies. The breakdown of important habitats which follows when traditional land-uses are replaced with unsustainable, tourist-based industries will inevitably lead to a silent dawn.

I am determined to do everything in my power to ensure that the generations of my children, grandchildren and far beyond, have the chance to observe, enjoy and marvel at the wildlife and its habitat with which I have been involved all my life.